THE NEW MERMAIDS

The Importance of Being Earnest

THE NEW MERMAIDS

General Editor

BRIAN GIBBONS

Professor of English Literature, University of Zürich

Previous general editors of the series have been:
PHILIP BROCKBANK
BRIAN MORRIS
ROMA GILL

MONCRIEFFE, CECILY, AND WORTHING.

WORTHING : *"Nothing will induce me to take his hand!"*

Allen Aynesworth, Evelyn Millard and George Alexander: studio photograph by Alfred Ellis of characters in the first production.
(Reproduced from the *Sketch*, 20 March 1895)

The Importance of Being Earnest

A Trivial Comedy for Serious People

OSCAR WILDE

Edited by
RUSSELL JACKSON
Fellow of the Shakespeare Institute,
University of Birmingham

LONDON/A & C BLACK

NEW YORK/W W NORTON

Third impression 1990
Published by A & C Black (Publishers) Limited
35 Bedford Row, London WC1R 4JH

First published in this form 1980 by Ernest Benn Limited

Introduction and text of notes © Ernest Benn Limited 1980
Appendices I, II and III and quotations from unpublished
drafts in notes © the Estate of Vyvyan Holland 1957

Published in the United States of America by
W W Norton and Company, Inc.
500 Fifth Avenue, New York, NY 10110

Printed in Great Britain by
Richard Clay Ltd, Bungay, Suffolk

British Library Cataloguing in Publication Data

Wilde, Oscar
    The importance of being earnest.—(New mermaids)
    I. Title   II. Jackson, Russell Bennett
    III. Series
    822'.8   PR5818.14

ISBN 0–7136–3040–X
ISBN 0–393–90045–2 (U.S.A.)

CONTENTS

ACKNOWLEDGEMENTS

I AM GRATEFUL to Mr Merlin Holland, the author's grandson, for permission to quote from manuscripts, typescripts, and proofs of *The Importance of Being Earnest*, and to the following institutions for access to materials in their possession: Birmingham Reference Library; the British Library; the British Theatre Museum; Harvard Theatre Collection; the Humanities Research Center, University of Texas; the New York Public Library. I am also indebted to Sir Rupert Hart-Davis and Mrs Eva Reichmann for permission to quote from annotations in Max Beerbohm's copy of the first edition of the play.

I have received much help and encouragement from friends and colleagues in Birmingham and elsewhere, particularly Linda Rosenberg, Tony Brown, and Ian Small. Joseph Donohue and Ruth Berggren have been generous with suggestions, information, and commiseration. I look forward eagerly to the publication of the results of their investigation of the text's composition, performance, and publication.

The Shakespeare Institute,   R.J.
1979

I have taken the opportunity of a reprint to correct errors and to add to the list of Further Reading (pages xlvii–xlviii).

1988   R.J.

ABBREVIATIONS

REFERENCES to *The Importance of Being Earnest* are to the line-numbers of the present edition. References to *The Picture of Dorian Gray* are to Isobel Murray's edition in the Oxford English Novels series (1974). Other works by Wilde are referred to by the title of the volume in which they appear in Ross's edition of the *Works* (14 vols., 1908). I have followed Murray's practice of giving additional references to the page-numbers of the Collins *Complete Works* (1967), which is designated *CW*. The following abbreviations are used to designate texts of *The Importance of Being Earnest* cited in the collations:

MS draft	The manuscript drafts of the four acts (August 1894) as transcribed in Volume I of Sarah Augusta Dickson, ed., *The Importance of Being Earnest . . . In Four Acts as Originally Written by Oscar Wilde* (New York Public Library: publication number 6 of the Arents Tobacco Collection, 2 vols., 1956). Acts I and II are in the Arents Collection, New York Public Library: Acts III and IV in the British Library.
Arents I, III, IV	Typescripts of Acts I, III, and IV, now in the Arents Collection, reproduced in collotype facsimile in Volume II of Dickson's edition.
OCT	Typescript of four-act version, dated 31 October 1894: Burnside-Frohman Collection, New York Public Library at Lincoln Center (+ NCOF 1894).
LC	Licensing Copy, British Library MS Add. 53567 (17) (*Lady Lancing. A Serious Comedy for Trivial People by Oscar Wilde*).
HTC/HTC1	Typescript owned by George Alexander: Harvard Theatre Collection. Where Alexander has made manuscript alterations, the original state of the typescript is referred to as HTC1.
WD	Typescript (typed by Winifred Dolan) revised by Wilde to provide copy for 1899: Arents Tobacco Collection, New York Public Library.
PR	Page-proofs of the 1899 edition, with Wilde's autograph alterations: manuscripts section of

	the Humanities Research Center, University of Texas, Austin, Texas.
1899	*The Importance of Being Earnest, A Trivial Comedy for Serious People by the Author of 'Lady Windermere's Fan'* (London, Leonard Smithers, 1899).
French's 1903	*The Importance of Being Earnest, A Trivial Comedy for Serious People in Three Acts by Oscar Wilde* (London, Samuel French, n.d. [1903]): French's Acting Edition, number 1036.

Other Abbreviations

om.   omits
s.d.   stage direction(s)

INTRODUCTION

THE AUTHOR

ANDRÉ GIDE DESCRIBES Oscar Wilde as he appeared in 1891, when 'his success was so certain that it seemed that it preceded [him] and that all he needed do was go forward and meet it':

> ... He was rich; he was tall; he was handsome; laden with good fortune and honours. Some compared him to an Asiatic Bacchus; others to some Roman emperor; others to Apollo himself—and the fact is that he was radiant.[1]

The melodramatic contrast between this triumphant figure and the pathetic convict serving two years' hard labour was drawn by Wilde himself in *De Profundis*, the letter written from prison to his lover, Lord Alfred Douglas. He described his transfer in November 1895 from Wandsworth to Reading Gaol, little care being taken for his privacy:

> From two o'clock till half-past two on that day I had to stand on the centre platform at Clapham Junction in convict dress and handcuffed, for the world to look at. I had been taken out of the Hospital Ward without a moment's notice being given to me. Of all possible objects I was the most grotesque. When people saw me they laughed. Each train as it came up swelled the audience. Nothing could exceed their amusement. That was of course before they knew who I was. As soon as they had been informed, they laughed still more. For half an hour I stood there in the grey November rain surrounded by a jeering mob.[2]

Wilde insisted that his life was as much an artistic endeavour as his works—in *De Profundis* he claimed to have been 'a man who stood in symbolic relations to the art and culture of my age', and in conversation with Gide he remarked that the great drama of his life lay in his having put his talent into his works, and his genius into his life.[3] For an author who returned as often as Wilde to the

---

[1] André Gide, 'In Memoriam' from *Oscar Wilde*, translated Bernard Frechtman (New York, 1949): quoted from the extract in Richard Ellmann, ed., *Oscar Wilde: a Collection of Critical Essays* (Englewood Cliffs, N.J., 1969), pp. 25–34. The principal sources for the present account of Wilde's career are H. Montgomery Hyde, *Oscar Wilde* (1975) and Rupert Hart-Davis, ed., *The Letters of Oscar Wilde* (revised ed., 1963). Subsequent references to Wilde's *Letters* are to this edition.

[2] Wilde, *Letters*, pp. 490–1. This long letter was written in Reading Gaol in January–March 1897. An abridged version was published by Robert Ross in 1905 as *De Profundis*: the most reliable edition is that contained in *Letters*, pp. 423–511.

[3] Wilde, *Letters*, p. 466; Gide, 'In Memoriam', ed. cit., p. 34.

proposition that art transforms and is the superior of Nature, such claims were more than boasting—they were an affirmation of faith.

Oscar Wilde was born in Dublin on 16 October 1854, second son of Sir William and Lady Wilde. The father was an eminent surgeon, the mother a poetess and fervent Irish nationalist who wrote as 'Speranza'. To medical distinction Sir William joined notoriety as a philanderer.[4] Both parents were enthusiasts for the study of Irish legend, folk-lore, and history, an interest reflected in the first two of the names given to their son, Oscar Fingal O'Flahertie Wills Wilde. He was educated at Portora Royal School and Trinity College, Dublin, where he became a protégé of the classicist John Pentland Mahaffy. In 1875 he won a scholarship—a 'Classical Demyship'—to Magdalen College, Oxford, where he subsequently took first-class honours in the final school of *Literae Humaniores* (Greek and Roman literature, history, and philosophy). He picked up a reputation for wit, charm, and conversational prowess. Most important, he came under the influence of two eminent writers on art and its relation to life, John Ruskin and Walter Pater. Ruskin, the most distinguished contemporary art critic, championed the moral and social dimensions of art, and its ability to influence men's lives for the better. Under Ruskin's supervision, Wilde and a few other undergraduates had begun the construction of a road near Hinksey, as a practical demonstration of the aesthetic dignity of labour and the workmanlike qualities essential to the labours of the artist. From Pater, Wilde learned a conflicting interpretation of art as a means to the cultivation of the individual, an idea which received its most notorious statement in the 'Conclusion' to Pater's book *The Renaissance*. There the fully-developed sensibility is claimed as the expression of a full existence: 'To burn always with this hard, gem-like flame, to maintain this ecstasy, is success in life'.[5] These two theories of the relation between art and life were to dominate Wilde's writing. The arguments of the painter James McNeill Whistler against the conservative critics' insistence on moral significance and pictorial verisimilitude in art also influenced Wilde deeply.[6] The close of his Oxford career was marked by two triumphs—his first-class degree

---

[4] On Sir William and Lady Wilde see Terence de Vere White, *Parents of Oscar Wilde* (1967).

[5] Walter Pater, *The Renaissance* (1873; Library ed., 1910), p. 236. This 'Conclusion' was omitted in the second edition (1877) and restored, in a modified form, in the third edition (1888).

[6] Whistler later quarrelled with Wilde, accusing him of plagiarism. Some of their exchanges appeared in Whistler's *The Gentle Art of Making Enemies* (1890) and in *Wilde vs. Whistler* (1906).

and the Newdigate Prize for his poem 'Ravenna'—and two fail-ures. Wilde was not given the Chancellor's English Essay Prize for his essay 'The Rise of Historical Criticism' and he was not offered a fellowship at Magdalen.

Moving to London, Wilde set about making himself a name in the capital's fashionable artistic and literary worlds. He had enough poems to make a collected volume, published at his own expense in 1881, and he was seen at the right parties, first nights, and private views. Occasionally he wore the velvet coat and knee-breeches, soft-collared shirt and cravat, that became fixed in the popular imagination as 'aesthetic' dress (and which derived from a fancy-dress ball he had attended when an undergraduate). In December 1881 he embarked on a lecture-tour of the United States organized by the impresario Richard D'Oyly Carte. This was a shrewd back-up to the tour of Gilbert and Sullivan's comic opera *Patience*, but it was also a simple exploitation of the American appetite for being lectured to. Although *Patience*, which satirized the Aesthetic Movement, featured rival poets dressed in a costume closely resembling that adopted by Wilde, the lecturer was taken seriously as a prophet of the 'new renaissance' of art. In his lectures he insisted on comparing the new preoccupation with life-styles with the aspirations of the Italian Renaissance and the Romantic Movement—this was 'a sort of new birth of the spirit of man', like the earlier rebirth 'in its desire for a more gracious and comely way of life, its passion for physical beauty, its exclusive attention to form, its seeking for new subjects for poetry, new forms of art, new intellectual and imaginative enjoyments . . .'[7] The blend of aesthe-tic theory and enthusiasm for reform of design and colouring in dress and decorative art was derived from a variety of sources, not all successfully synthesized. In addition to Ruskin, Pater, and Whistler, Wilde had absorbed the ideas of William Morris and the architect E. W. Godwin. The lectures were exercises in *haute vulgarisation* and not all the sources were acknowledged. Japanese and other oriental art, eighteenth-century furniture, distempered walls in pastel colours, stylized floral motifs—all had made their appearance in English art before Wilde became their advocate. But the influence of his popularizing talents was, for all that, consider-able. 'In fact', wrote Max Beerbohm in 1895, looking back on 1880 as though it were a remote historical period, 'Beauty had existed long before 1880. It was Mr Oscar Wilde who managed her *début*'.[8]

As well as establishing him as a popular oracle on matters of art

[7] Wilde, 'The English Renaissance of Art', in Ross's edition of his *Essays and Lectures* (1909), pp. 111–55; pp. 111f. The text was edited by Ross from four drafts of a lecture first given in New York on 9 January 1882.

[8] Max Beerbohm, *Works* (1896; 'collected' edition, 1922, p. 39).

and taste, Wilde's lecture-tour made him a great deal of badly-needed money—he had no prospect of inheriting a family fortune, and would have to make his own way. On his return the velvet suits were discarded, and his hair, worn long and flowing in his 'Aesthetic' period, was cut short in a style resembling the young Nero. The figure described by Gide was beginning to emerge. After a holiday in Paris, Wilde moved into rooms at 9 Charles Street, Grosvenor Square. He returned briefly to New York for the first performance of his melodrama *Vera; or the Nihilists* and then prepared for an autumn lecture-tour of the United Kingdom. On 26 November he became engaged to Constance Lloyd, and they married on 29 May 1884. In January 1885 they moved into a house designed by Godwin at 16 Tite Street, Chelsea. Two sons, Cyril and Vyvyan, were born in 1885 and 1886 respectively. In the early years of his marriage Wilde was working hard as a journalist. He contributed reviews to magazines (including the *Pall Mall Gazette* and the *Dramatic World*) and even for a while undertook the editorship of one, *Woman's World*, which he hoped to turn into 'the recognized organ through which women of culture and position will express their views, and to which they will contribute'.[9] By and by Constance came into a small inheritance, but money was never plentiful. The life of a professional journalist was laborious and demanded a high degree of craftsmanship, but it offered a training from which Wilde, like Shaw, Wells, and many others, profited immensely. Wilde became a fastidious and tireless reviser of his own work, and his reviews show him as an acute critic of others.

In 1891 four of Wilde's books appeared, all consisting of earlier work, some of it in a revised form: *Intentions*, a collection of critical essays; *Lord Arthur Saville's Crime and Other Stories*; *The Picture of Dorian Gray*, considerably altered from the version published in *Lippincott's Magazine* in 1890; and a collection of children's stories, *A House of Pomegranates*. In the same year a verse tragedy written in 1882, *The Duchess of Padua*, was produced in New York by Lawrence Barrett under the title *Guido Ferranti*. Like *Vera* it was poorly received, but Wilde was already turning away from the pseudo-Elizabethan dramatic form that had preoccupied so many nineteenth-century poets and contemplating a newer, more commercially acceptable mode. In the summer of 1891 he began work on the first of a series of successful plays for the fashionable theatres of the West End: *Lady Windermere's Fan* (St James's, 20 February 1892), *A Woman of No Importance* (Haymarket, 19 April 1893), and *An Ideal Husband* (Haymarket, 3 January 1895). The refusal of a performance licence to the exotic biblical tragedy *Salomé* (in 1892)

[9] Wilde, *Letters*, p. 202 (to Mrs Alfred Hunt, August 1887).

proved a temporary setback: acclaim as a dramatic author confirmed Wilde's career in what seemed an irresistible upward curve.

The summer of 1891 was also remarkable for the beginning of an association that was to be the direct cause of his downfall: the poet Lionel Johnson introduced him to 'Bosie', Lord Alfred Douglas, third son of the Marquis of Queensberry. Wilde appears to have been already a practising homosexual, and his marriage was under some strain. The affair with Douglas estranged him further from Constance, and the drain it caused on Wilde's nervous and financial resources was formidable. Douglas was happy to let Wilde spend money on him after his father had stopped his allowance: more seriously, he made ceaseless demands on the time set aside for writing. In *De Profundis* Wilde described his attempts to finish *An Ideal Husband* in an apartment in St James's Place:

> I arrived . . . every morning at 11.30, in order to have the opportunity of thinking and writing without the interruptions inseparable from my own household, quiet and peaceful as that household was. But the attempt was vain. At twelve o'clock you drove up, and stayed smoking cigarettes and chattering till 1.30, when I had to take you out to luncheon at the Café Royal or the Berkeley. Luncheon with its *liqueurs* lasted usually till 3.30. For an hour you retired to White's [Club]. At tea-time you appeared again, and stayed until it was time to dress for dinner. You dined with me either at the Savoy or at Tite Street. We did not separate as a rule till after midnight, as supper at Willis's had to wind up the entrancing day.[10]

This was in 1893. A year later Wilde was working on what was to prove his last play, *The Importance of Being Earnest*, the first draft of which had been composed during a family holiday (largely Douglas-free) at Worthing. In October, Constance had returned to London with the children. Wilde and Douglas stayed together in Brighton, first at the Metropole Hotel, then in private lodgings. Douglas developed influenza and Wilde nursed him through it. He in turn suffered an attack of the virus, and Douglas (by Wilde's account) more or less neglected him. The result was what seemed like an irrevocable quarrel, with Douglas living at Wilde's expense in a hotel but hardly bothering to visit him. In hindsight Wilde claimed that this cruelty afforded him a moment of clear understanding:

> Is it necessary for me to state that I saw clearly that it would be a dishonour to myself to continue even an acquaintance with such a one as you had showed [*sic*] yourself to be? That I recognized that ultimate moment had come, and recognized it as being really a great relief? And

10 Wilde, *Letters*, p. 426.

that I knew that for the future my Art and Life would be freer and better and more beautiful in every possible way? Ill as I was, I felt at ease.[11]

But reconciliation followed.

On 3 January 1895 *An Ideal Husband* was given its first performance. Meanwhile George Alexander, actor-manager of the St James's Theatre, had turned down the new comedy. It found a taker in Charles Wyndham, who intended to bring it out at the Criterion. Then Alexander found himself at a loss for a play to replace Henry James's *Guy Domville*, which had failed spectacularly. Wyndham agreed to release *The Importance of Being Earnest* on the condition that he had the option on Wilde's next play, and it was put into rehearsal at the St James's. At first Wilde attended rehearsals, but his continual interruptions made Alexander suggest that he might leave the manager and his company to their own resources. He agreed with good grace and left with Douglas for a holiday in Algeria. There they encountered André Gide, who was told by Wilde that he had a premonition of some disaster awaiting him on his return.[12] Although his artistic reputation was beyond question, and he was shortly to have two plays running simultaneously in the West End, Wilde was already worried by the activities of Douglas's father. Queensberry was a violent, irrational man, who hated his son's lover and was capable of hurting both parties. Bosie insisted on flaunting his relationship with Wilde to annoy his father and he was reckless of the effect of this public display of unconventional behaviour. Homosexuality was no less a fact of life in 1895 than it is now: moreover, the artistic and theatrical world accommodated it better than society at large. It had a flourishing and varied subculture and a number of sophisticated apologists. The double life that it entailed was by no means a simple matter of deceit and guilt for Wilde: it suited the cultivation of moral independence and detachment from society that he considered essential to art. None the less, if his affair with Douglas should ever come to be more public, and if the law were to be invoked, Wilde would be ruined. There had been scandals and trials involving homosexuals of the upper classes, which had to a degree closed their ranks to protect their own. But Wilde had made powerful enemies in a country whose leaders, institutions, and press seemed devoted to Philistinism and where art itself was always suspect as constituting a threat to the moral fibre of the

[11] Wilde, *Letters*, p. 438.

[12] 'I am not claiming that Wilde clearly saw prison rising up before him; but I do assert that the dramatic turn which surprised and astounded London, abruptly turning Wilde from accuser to accused, did not, strictly speaking, cause him any surprises' (Gide, 'In Memoriam', ed. cit., p. 34).

nation. *Dorian Gray* in particular had aroused violent mistrust, especially in its original form, and a satirical novel by Robert Hichens, *The Green Carnation* (1894), had hinted at a homosexual relationship between two characters obviously based on Wilde and Douglas. Queensberry had made his feelings about his son's private life well known in Clubland. On the first night of *The Importance of Being Earnest*, which opened on 14 February 1895, he tried to cause a disturbance at the theatre, but was thwarted by the management. The play was a great success—according to one of the actors, 'The audience rose in their seats and cheered and cheered again'.[13] As it settled down to what promised to be a long run, Wilde's career was at its height.

A fortnight later, on 28 February, Queensberry left a card at the Albemarle Club 'For Oscar Wilde posing as a somdomite' [*sic*]. The club porter put the card in an envelope, noting on the back the time and date, and Wilde was given it when he arrived at the club later that evening. The events that followed ruined him within a few months. Urged on by Douglas, but against the advice of most of his friends, Wilde sued Queensberry for criminal libel. The case went against Wilde, who found himself answering charges under the 1885 Criminal Law Amendment Act, which made both private and public homosexual relations between men illegal. Significantly, the accusations against him did not include his affair with Douglas: he was alleged to have committed acts of gross indecency on a number of occasions and to have conspired to procure the committing of such acts. The men involved were 'renters', young, lower-class, male prostitutes, and there was a strong sense in the proceedings that Wilde was being tried for betraying his class's social as well as sexual ethics. Much was made of the alleged immorality of his works, especially *Dorian Gray*. The jury at what was effectively the second trial of Wilde (after the hearings in his charge against Queensberry) failed to agree, and a retrial was ordered. Finally, on 25 May 1895, Wilde was convicted and sentenced to two years' imprisonment with hard labour. In the autumn he was declared bankrupt and all his effects were auctioned, including drafts and manuscripts of published and unpublished works. On 19 May 1897 he was released, and took up residence in France. During his imprisonment he had composed a long, bitter letter to Douglas, later published under the title *De Profundis*. Shortly after his release he completed a narrative poem, *The Ballad of Reading Gaol*. These and a few letters to the press on prison reform apart, Wilde published nothing new after his imprisonment. He did manage to

[13] Allen Aynesworth, quoted by Hesketh Pearson, *The Life of Oscar Wilde* (1946), p. 257.

arrange for the publication of *The Importance of Being Earnest* and *An Ideal Husband*, which appeared in 1899. Projects for further plays came to nothing. The affair with Douglas was taken up again and continued sporadically. They led a nomadic life on the continent, Wilde often chronically in debt despite the good offices of his friends. His allowance from Constance was withdrawn when he resumed living with Bosie. His plays were not yet being revived in England and his published works brought in little by way of royalties.

Wilde died on 30 November 1900 in Paris, from cerebral meningitis which set in after an operation on his ear. The day before he had been received into the Roman Catholic Church. He was buried at Bagneux, but in 1909 his remains were moved to the Père Lachaise cemetery, where they now rest under a monument by Jacob Epstein.

THE PLAY

Reviewing the first production of *The Importance of Being Earnest* William Archer asked what 'a poor critic' could do with a play that 'raises no principles, whether of art or morals, creates its own canons and conventions, and is nothing but an absolutely wilful expression of an irrepressibly witty personality'.[14] Another contemporary remarked that one might as well sit down gravely to discuss 'the true inwardness of a soufflé' and Max Beerbohm, in a notice of the 1902 revival, skilfully avoided defining the comedy: 'In kind the play always was unlike any other, and in its kind it still seems perfect'.[15] Despite the forcefulness of these claims, it is possible to see that Wilde's play does touch on principles of art and morals, and that it does have some relation to existing canons and conventions. Like a soufflé, it has its ingredients.

The St James's Theatre, where *The Importance of Being Earnest* was produced, was particularly associated with what was claimed to be a renaissance of dramatic art in England. Since November 1890 it had been under the management of the actor George Alexander, who had built up its reputation for stylish and accomplished productions of well-written plays. The St James's was identified with Alexander in a way almost unknown today but natural in a period when leading actors and actresses aspired to the management of a theatre and its company, and were expected to take the leading roles in the plays they produced. Alexander was

[14] William Archer, *The Theatrical 'World' of 1895* (1896), pp. 56–60; p. 57.

[15] Anonymous review, *Truth*, 21 February 1895. Max Beerbohm. *Around Theatres* (1953), pp. 188–91, p. 189.

unusually self-effacing in not insisting on this prerogative and in his readiness to accommodate as far as possible the author who wished to supervise the staging of his plays—although the ultimate authority lay with the manager in these days before the ascendancy of the independent director. He was disinclined to have plays altered to give undue prominence to the character he played, and treated his fellow-performers with the same courtesy he extended to authors, considering himself as a collaborator rather than a tyrant. Before 1895 his most notable successes at the St James's were R. C. Carton's farce *Liberty Hall* (December 1892), Pinero's drama *The Second Mrs Tanqueray* (May 1893) and Henry Arthur Jones's *The Masqueraders* (April 1894). A command performance of *Liberty Hall* before Queen Victoria consolidated the social standing of the theatre. In the words of Alexander's biographer, the playwright A. E. W. Mason,

> . . . Alexander was gradually gathering a regular band of theatre-goers at his theatre, people who must see the new play at the St James's whatever the newspapers said about it; people from the big houses in the suburbs as well as the artists, doctors, judges and dwellers in inner London who filled the stalls and dress-circle during the first performances.[16]

This audience was fashionable but not raffish, reflecting the theatre's location: near the West End without adjoining its less respectable areas; handy for Clubland in St James's and Pall Mall and the expensive houses and apartments of Mayfair and Belgravia.

Although he made successful forays into more romantic regions—including productions of *Much Ado about Nothing* and *As You Like It* and an adaptation of *The Prisoner of Zenda*—Alexander's repertoire was made up chiefly of plays domestic and upper-class (or upper-middle-class) in milieu, reflecting the status and tastes of his audience. He insisted on meticulously realistic settings that would serve rather than overshadow the author's intentions, and his audiences expected that good manners, taste, and the values of polite society would prevail on both sides of the curtain. His acting was skilful and subtle. Wilde singled him out for mention in a review of Irving's *Hamlet* published in 1885 when Alexander was acting in the Lyceum company: in his Laertes, Wilde saw evidence of 'a most effective presence . . . charming voice, and . . . capacity for wearing costumes with ease and

---

[16] A. E. W. Mason, *Sir George Alexander and the St James's Theatre* (1935), p. 97. See also Ray Mander and Joe Mitchenson, *Lost Theatres of London* (2nd ed., 1977); Paul C. Wadleigh, '*Earnest* at the St James's Theatre', *Quarterly Journal of Speech*, 52 (1966), 58–62; Joseph Donohue, 'The First Production of *The Importance of Being Earnest*: A Proposal for a Reconstructive Study' in Kenneth Richards and Peter Thomson, eds., *Nineteenth Century British Theatre* (1971), pp. 125–43.

elegance'.[17] Alexander retained the qualities of an attractive *jeune premier* well into middle age. His knighthood in 1911 seemed the appropriate honour for an actor of gentlemen.

Society Drama reflected the values of the stalls and dress-circles of the West End as accurately as Alexander's acting reflected upper-class standards of politeness and ease of address. It was a modification of the serious drama and domestic comedy of the mid-century decades. Melodrama survived at the Adelphi and Drury Lane, and at many suburban and provincial theatres, but its original preoccupations of kinship and personal guilt and innocence were increasingly overshadowed by ever more sophisticated representations of public events, famous sights, and natural or man-made disasters. Melodrama plots were progressing rapidly from the highly improbable to the practically impossible and its settings were drawn more often from 'high life'—however badly rendered—than from the middle- and lower-class background popular in earlier days.[18] Society Drama may be seen as an attempt to revive the virtues associated with melodrama in its best manifestations—its ability to move audiences, simplicity and directness of effect, combination of comic, didactic, and spectacular elements—and to produce a native drama that would be the rival, indeed superior, of French work. Arthur Wing Pinero, Henry Arthur Jones, and a number of other dramatists were attempting to do without spectacle and avoid gross improbabilities while keeping the 'strong' situations and moral clarity of the older plays. In comic writing the break with stock characterization associated with the plays of T. W. Robertson and the Bancrofts' management at the Prince of Wales's in the 1860s was now confirmed: but the setting of one class against (or beside) another, which provided the motive power of plays like Robertson's *Caste* (1867), was superseded by concern with the dynamics of characters *within* a particular class. Society Drama, serious, comic, and mixed, deals with the ways in which the ruling class policed itself.

The moral world of these plays is clearly defined. Between about 1885 and the Great War of 1914–18 there is a remarkable degree of agreement among playwrights in the commercial theatre as to what constitute the moral norms of Society, and what conflicts might arise between these and human weakness. The chief material

[17] Wilde, *'Hamlet* at the Lyceum', *Dramatic Review*, 9 May 1885.

[18] 'Society' in this context, with a capital 'S', refers to the values and fashions of the ruling élite, as distinct from the community ('society') at large. On Society Drama, see J. C. Trewin, *The Edwardian Theatre* (Oxford, Blackwell, 1976)—especially Chapter Two—and George Rowell, *The Victorian Theatre, 1792–1914* (2nd ed., Cambridge, 1978), which provides a useful bibliography. On the decline of melodrama, see Michael Booth, *English Melodrama* (1965), Chapters Six and Seven.

responsibilities of their class and their country are borne by men, on whose strength of character all depends. The man who makes nothing of his life can command no respect, and it is one of the principal functions of women to determine who merits respect and to make their discrimination apparent in their choice of whom to marry. Women set the spiritual tone, and without a supply of good women, Society will crumble. Camilla, the title-character of Pinero's *Lady Bountiful* (Garrick, 1891) makes this clear to her feckless cousin Dennis Heron:

> ... Dennis, it isn't great men women love dearest, or even fortunate men; often, I tell you, their deepest love goes out to those who labour and fail. But for those who make no effort, who are neither great nor little, who are the nothings of the world ... For those, a true woman has only one feeling—anger and contempt![19]

Such men might behave in a mean or unmanly way, and will need the support of a good woman if they are to redeem themselves. In Jones's *The Triumph of the Philistines* (which followed *The Importance of Being Earnest* at the St James's in May 1895) Lady Beauboys pleads with Mrs Suleny to help such a reprobate:

> Do take pity on him! He'll go to the dogs if you don't. Remember what we women are sent into this world for—remember there is no reason for our existence except to save these poor wretches of men from following their natural bent of going to the dogs. Do save him.[20]

Such is to be Cecily's mission in helping the wicked Ernest to reform himself.[21] If a man meets a bad woman, her influence is likely to have the opposite effect. In Hubert Henry Davies's comedy *Mrs Gorringe's Necklace* (Wyndham's, 1903) David Cairns is desperately in need of his fiancée's help—unbeknown to her he has stolen a necklace that belongs to a fellow house-guest. He suggests bitterly that he is not worthy of her, but she insists, 'Suppose you loved a bad woman?'

> How could I bear to see you dragged down by a bad woman, knowing that I might have saved you? (*Goes to him with a sudden impulse, kneels beside him and puts her arms about him*) David! David! You must try—try hard—for my sake.[22]

She marries him, still unaware of his guilt, and a friend decides to take the blame for David's crime in order to spare her the shame of

---

[19] A. W. Pinero, *Lady Bountiful* (1891), p. 37.
[20] Henry Arthur Jones, *The Triumph of the Philistines* (1899), p. 93.
[21] *The Importance of Being Earnest*, II, 159–65. (This and all subsequent references are to the line-numbers of the present edition.)
[22] Hubert Henry Davies, *Mrs Gorringe's Necklace* (1910), p. 49.

his unmasking. David, however, pre-empts the friend's chivalry by shooting himself.

A less drastic means of reforming the man who has erred is emigration. Active service in the colonies, farming in New Zealand or Australia, and even mining and general pioneering in North America will clear a man's mind and give him a fresh view of Society. This kind of experience is often used to establish character—as in the case of Gunning in Haddon Chambers's *The Tyranny of Tears* (Criterion, 1899), who has been adventuring in Upper India, and has done 'a rather fine thing . . . saved a lot of miserable lives—an ordinary, manly, commonplace, heroic, English sort of thing'.[23] The colonies assume the pastoral virtues traditionally associated with the countryside and serve as a useful contrast with the city. In Alfred Sutro's *The Walls of Jericho* (Garrick, 1903), Jack Frobisher, having made his fortune sheep-farming in Queensland, has come back to marry a Society beauty in London. She falls in with a fast set of wives who play bridge for a shilling a point, run up debts, and flirt with other men ('All the women we know', she explains, 'call the men by their Christian names'). Hankey Bannister, a friend newly arrived from Australia, puts the choice frankly before Frobisher: 'Which will you be—the Man of Queensland or the Gentleman of Mayfair?'[24] Frobisher wavers, but the discovery of his wife in a compromising situation with a known philanderer decides him. He will take his child and go back to the sheep. At first defiant, his wife relents in the final moments of the play and agrees to accompany him to a new life. As well as possessing this figurative significance, the colonies are of great practical use to dramatists who want to get rid of characters or introduce them suddenly. The device had worked well for a long time, in melodrama and elsewhere, although the old business of the transported criminal's return (exemplified by Magwitch in *Great Expectations*) no longer served.

The kind of conduct that might necessitate a tour of duty abroad (or even permanent exile) is made clear by Pinero's Aubrey Tanqueray in his angry denunciation of 'a man's life'. Hugh Ardale, suitor for the hand of Tanqueray's daughter Ellean, led in younger days a dissolute life, went to India to recover his moral stamina, and acted valorously there. Ellean has heard Ardale's confession of his past sins, and has forgiven him, but neither of them realize that Ellean's stepmother, the 'Second Mrs Tanqueray' of the title, once had a liaison with Ardale. Pinero makes it plain that even a good woman's forgiveness cannot always put right the

[23] C. Haddon Chambers, *The Tyranny of Tears*, ed. Michael Booth, *English Plays of the Nineteenth Century, III: Comedies* (Oxford, 1973), pp. 412–13.
[24] Alfred Sutro, *The Walls of Jericho* (1906), p. 49.

consequences of past evil or cut away the tangle of deceit for which both man and woman are equally responsible. Aubrey Tanqueray has himself acted recklessly in marrying a woman 'with a past' and recognizes Ardale's behaviour as consistent with a pattern:

> He has only led 'a man's life'—just as I, how many of us, have done! The misery he has brought on me and mine it's likely enough we, in our own time, have helped to bring on others by this leading 'a man's life' . . .[25]

The man who marries a woman whose reputation is not secure faces a life of social ostracism, possibly exile. Although his male friends will not openly shun him, they are not likely to allow his wife to meet their wives or daughters—the very presence of a bad woman was offensive to the good.[26] As for the man who marries a good woman without confessing his past, he is likely to find himself unmasked in the fifth act. In *The Profligate* Pinero sets up as target an outspoken defender of the double standard, Lord Dungars, who replies to an upright Scots lawyer's insistence that the husband who does not admit all 'wrongs his wife and fools himself':

> Why, my dear Mr Murray, you're actually putting men on a level with ladies. Ladies, I admit, are like nations—to be happy they should have no histories. But don't you know that Marriage is the tomb of the past, as far as a man is concerned?

Later in the play a conversation between two of the women leaves no doubt as to the author's sympathies: a man's past is his wife's 'pride or her shame, the jewel she wears upon her brow or the mud which clings to her skirts! It is her light or her darkness: her life or her death!'[27] The attack on a man's right to 'sow his wild oats' carried the implication not that men and women alike should be pardoned, but that both should be equally punished. This is the plea of Hester in *A Woman of No Importance*: 'Set a mark, if you wish on each . . .'[28] But this was a radical suggestion, and the

[25] A. W. Pinero, *The Second Mrs Tanqueray*, ed. George Rowell, *Late Victorian Plays* (1968), pp. 1–79; p. 79. The speech occurs in the final act, just before Ellean tells Tanqueray (and the audience) that Paula has killed herself—another victim of 'a man's life'.

[26] Readers of *Manners and Rules of Good Society . . . By a Member of the Aristocracy* (32nd ed., 1910) are warned against the casual acquaintanceships that might be picked up without formal introduction by English people abroad, who might not be aware that they had encountered an exile 'perhaps well bred and agreeable, although tabooed at home for some good and sufficient reason'. It was painful for kind-hearted travellers when they were 'subsequently compelled to avoid and to relinquish the acquaintance of those with whom they [had] become pleasantly intimate' (p. 66).

[27] A. W. Pinero, *The Profligate* (1891), pp. 5; 57.

[28] *A Woman of No Importance*, p. 72/*CW*, p. 450. Wilde was himself the victim of a 'double standard' implicit in the Criminal Law Amendment Act, 1885, which dealt exclusively with relations between men.

wisdom of the world maintained that men could get away with adventures absolutely forbidden to women. In Jones's *The Case of Rebellious Susan* (Criterion, 1894) a woman decides to pay back in his own coin a husband who has been paying attention to other women. She gets no further than flirtation, and reconciliation is effected through the good offices of Sir Richard Kato, a *raisonneur* of the kind that the actor Charles Wyndham excelled in. In the first act Kato warns Susan:

> My dear Sue, believe me, what is sauce for the goose will never be sauce for the gander. In fact, there is no gander sauce, eh, Lady Derby?[29]

Wyndham was concerned that the play might be judged flippant or indecent, and wrote Jones a long cautionary letter while he was working on it:

> The tendency of the drama should always, if possible, be elevating. If we depart from this ever, as in the case of Mrs Tanqueray, and such like, the subject has to be grappled with seriously.[30]

The presence of a *raisonneur* like Kato was a guarantee against this—he might even act as a detective in the police-force guarding Society, unearthing past indiscretions before they can cause harm (as Kato does) or even interrogating a suspect, as Sir Daniel Carteret interrogates Mrs Dane in Jones's *Mrs Dane's Defence* (Wyndham's, 1900) to find out whether she is indeed unfit for good Society.[31]

A dramatic form in which so much depended upon discriminations and the concept of 'Society', and in which the settings and characters were almost exclusively upper-class might be expected to appeal to Wilde. But the emphasis on moral judgements was less attractive to one who favoured the substitution of aesthetic for ethical values. The three Society plays reflect this, as well as a lack of sympathy with some of the practical conventions of the *genre*.

[29] Henry Arthur Jones, *The Case of Rebellious Susan* (1897), p. 8.

[30] Charles Wyndham, letter to Jones quoted by Doris Arthur Jones, *The Life and Letters of Henry Arthur Jones* (1930), pp. 166–7. Cf. the account of Pinero's ambitions in M. C. Salaman's 'Introductory Note' to *The Profligate* (1891): Pinero hopes to write 'plays which should, by means of a simple and reasonable dramatic deduction, record actual experience flowing in the natural irregular rhythm of life, which should at the same time embody lofty ideals of conduct and character.' (p.v.)

[31] *Mrs Dane's Defence* is available in Michael Booth, ed., *The Magistrate and Other Plays* (1974) and the second volume (1969) of the same editor's *English Plays of the Nineteenth Century*.

Lady Windermere's Fan, A Woman of No Importance, and *An Ideal Husband* all deal with indiscretions that have been or must be concealed. In the first Mrs Erlynne, a woman with a 'past', is making her entry into Society with the help of Lord Windermere: her secret is that she is Lady Windermere's mother. In *A Woman of No Importance* Mrs Arbuthnot urges her son not to accept the advancement in his career that Lord Illingworth offers him, but she cannot tell him her reason: he is illegitimate and Illingworth is his father. Sir Robert Chiltern, in *An Ideal Husband*, is a cabinet minister whose career was launched on the proceeds of disclosing information to one Baron Arnheim, a sinister foreign profiteer. Chiltern cannot admit this to his wife and he is being blackmailed by an adventuress (with a selection of pasts) called Mrs Cheveley. In all three plays the background is one of receptions, balls, and house parties, which give Wilde the chance to write witty dialogue appropriate to the kind of social occasion at which he himself shone, but the plots need serious confrontations to propel the characters through the necessary moral dilemmas, and here he is less happy. The affinity he feels with a brilliant and dominating personality makes him write tellingly for Lord Illingworth when nothing important is happening, and lapse into stiff, melodramatic mannerisms when a crisis has to be dealt with. As Ian Gregor has remarked, 'The more Illingworth moves into the plot, the less Wilde cares about what he says'.[32] Other dramatists were happy to write the occasional impassioned, rhetorical, somewhat old-fashioned speech, but Wilde's distrust of cant makes him give Hester, in *A Woman of No Importance*, an impressive harangue on the double standard of morality, and then undercut it with the witty and blithely complacent reaction of the Englishwomen she is addressing:

> ... And till you count what is a shame in a woman to be infamy in a man, you will always be unjust, and Right, that pillar of fire, and Wrong, that pillar of cloud, will be made dim to your eyes, or not be seen at all, or if seen, not regarded.

LADY CAROLINE
> Might I, my dear Miss Worsley, as you are standing up, ask you for my cotton that is just behind you? Thank you.[33]

Nonchalance is more congenial to Wilde than enthusiasm. In *An Ideal Husband* he finds an integral function for his preferred attitude by making a dandy, Lord Goring, the *raisonneur*, in place

---

[32] Ian Gregor, 'Comedy and Oscar Wilde', *Sewanee Review*, 74 (1966), 501–21; p. 508. See also Arthur Ganz, 'The Divided Self in the Society Comedies of Oscar Wilde', *Modern Drama*, 3 (1960), 16–23.

[33] Cf. note 28, above.

of the usual lawyer, doctor, or avuncular 'man of the world'.
Goring finds the solution to Chiltern's dilemma, but maintains his
detachment. He is intolerant of the public's regard for morality:

> ... in England a man who can't talk morality twice a week to a large,
> popular, immoral audience is quite over as a serious politician. There
> would be nothing left for him as a profession except Botany or the
> Church.[34]

By making Chiltern a *man* with a past Wilde is able to invert the
clichés associated with a moral situation without forfeiting its
validity in the scheme of the play. He has Chiltern reproach his
wife in terms familiar from discussions of her own sex: 'Why can't
you women love us, faults and all? Why do you place us on
monstrous pedestals?' It was in this speech that Shaw recognized
the 'modern note' of the play.[35]

From the preliminary scheme for a serious drama that he sent
Alexander in the summer of 1894 it is clear that Wilde was looking
for new ways of handling the materials appropriate to success in the
commercial theatre. *Salomé* had been banned by the Lord Chamberlain in 1892, on the grounds that it represented Biblical characters: that kind of experiment was clearly not going to find a place in
the West End and certainly would not make money. The new
serious play was never written by Wilde, although Frank Harris
later worked up a drama, *Mr and Mrs Daventry*, along the lines
indicated in the proposals. It was to show a 'man of rank and
fashion' married to 'a simple sweet country girl—a lady—but
simple and ignorant of fashionable life'.[36] The man would become
bored, and would invite 'a lot of fashionable *fin-de-siècle* men and
women' to stay. Among them would be Gerald Lancing, with
whom the wife would be allowed to flirt. The husband would
himself flirt with a Lady X, and the wife would fall in love with
Lancing. The final scene would depict the triumph of love: the
husband would shoot himself, leaving Gerald and the wife 'cling-
ing to each other as if with a mad desire to make love eternal'. Wilde
assured Alexander that he thought this was 'extremely strong'.

> ... I want the sheer passion of love to dominate everything. No morbid
> self-sacrifice. No renunciation. A sheer flame of love between a man and
> a woman.

---

[34] *An Ideal Husband*, p. 86/*CW*, p. 507.

[35] *An Ideal Husband*, p. 133/*CW*, p. 521.

[36] Wilde, *Letters*, pp. 360–2. Harris's play has been published with an introduction
by H. Montgomery Hyde (1956).

This was to be a modern tragedy, and it is clear from Wilde's outline that the love of Gerald and the wife was to be shown developing in the course of the play, rather than exist already as some secret to be unearthed in the conventional way. The contrast of simplicity and sophistication is there in the wife and her husband's friends, and the passionate sexuality tentatively explored in *Salomé* is to be the dominating force.

The summer of 1894 also produced a parallel comic scheme for developing and transcending the conventions of the theatre: *The Importance of Being Earnest*. In this everything depends upon the rediscovery of the past, and the appropriate material exhibits are produced in evidence: a cigarette-case, a hand-bag, the Army Lists of the last forty years. The credentials of a prospective son-in-law are checked and the grounds of his admissibility to Society are investigated. A scapegrace is to be rescued by a good woman from the alternatives of the next world and Australia. Innocence is set against sophistication, the country against the town, in the persons of Cecily and Gwendolen ('A girl with a simple, unspoiled nature', who 'could hardly be expected to reside in the country'; I, 518–19). The audience is kept aware of the dictates of Divine justice ('As a man sows so let him reap'; II, 37) and its poetic equivalent ('The good ended happily, and the bad unhappily. That is what Fiction means'; II, 54–5). The play ends with the promise of three weddings and the discovery of kinship between two of the bridegrooms.

Wilde uses this material to create neither a straightforward dramatic parody—that would have been nothing new—nor a farcical comedy of the kind written by Brandon Thomas (*Charley's Aunt*) or Pinero (*Dandy Dick*, *The Magistrate*, *The Schoolmistress*). His characters do not collide with the real world, but are endowed with an enviable control over it. Their rare moments of helplessness are enjoyed as though they had wished them upon themselves—'The suspense is terrible', says Gwendolen as Jack searches for the hand-bag, 'I hope it will last' (III, 387). Parts of the play are written with a quasi-operatic formality that makes the characters appear as Wilde's collaborators. The tea-table scene between Cecily and Gwendolen, their joint confrontation of the two men, and the opening sequence of Act III are composed in this manner. The speakers cap each other's lines, rhythm for rhythm and word for word. When Gwendolen observes, '*meditatively*',

> If the poor fellow has been entrapped into any foolish promise I shall consider it my duty to rescue him at once, and with a firm hand,

Cecily announces her own resolution, '*thoughtfully and sadly*',

> Whatever unfortunate entanglement my dear boy may have got into, I
> will never reproach him with it after we are married.
>
> $(II, 664–9)^{37}$

In the earlier Society plays of Wilde the necessity of using such
language was an embarrassing duty: here it has become a pleasure.
Jack's speech of forgiveness when he thinks Miss Prism is his
mother is the most striking example:

> Unmarried! I do not deny that is a serious blow. But after all, who has
> the right to cast a stone against one who has suffered? Cannot repentance
> wipe out an act of folly? Why should there be one law for men, and
> another for women? Mother, I forgive you.
>
> $(III, 406–10)$

It is appropriate that Jack should invoke Christ's words on the
woman taken in adultery, as Miss Prism herself has used a sterner
judgement derived from St Paul—'As a man sows, so let him reap'.
For a moment we are reminded of the most pathetic of Victorian
wronged women, Lady Isabel Vane in *East Lynne*, who returned
disguised as a governess from an exile in which she was thought to
have died, to watch over the death bed of a son who expired without
having called her 'mother'.[38] Wilde uses this kind of effect spar-
ingly, just as serious dramas of the new school avoided excessive
reliance on techniques associated with melodrama.

The Importance of Being Earnest also observes a degree of
decorum in characterization, keeping well away from the stock
types. Neither Jack nor Algernon speaks with the ebullient raciness
of the stage 'swell' or the slangy drawl of the dim theatrical younger
son. Aynesworth, who played Algernon, was well known for his
'clever impersonations of masherdom',[39] and a comparison of the
lines Wilde gave him with a specimen from Pinero's *The Weaker Sex*
(Royal Court, 1889) shows how little the new play owed to popular
comic cliché. In Pinero's play Aynesworth appeared as the Hon.
George Liptrott, idle, rich, and vacant. In this speech he is telling
his mother about one of the other guests at an evening party:

---

[37] W. H. Auden suggested that the play is 'the only pure verbal opera in English'
('An Improbable Life', *New Yorker*, 9 March 1963—reprinted by Ellmann, *Oscar
Wilde: a Collection of Critical Essays*, pp. 116–37). On the formal qualities of the play
(especially the second act), cf. Otto Reinert, 'The Courtship Dance in *The Importance of Being Earnest*', *Modern Drama*, 1 (1959), 256–7.

[38] Mrs Henry Wood's novel *East Lynne* (published in book form in 1861) was
dramatized a number of times: T. A. Palmer's version (1874) is reprinted by
Leonard R. N. Ashley, *Nineteenth Century British Drama* (Glenview, Ill., 1967).
The most famous line occurs at the end of Act Three: 'Oh, Willie, my child dead,
dead, dead! and he never knew me, never called me mother' (p. 390).

[39] *The Dramatic Peerage* (1895).

Why, Ma, that's Wade Green, the man who's so awfully entertaining at the piano with those frightfully amusing songs—don't you know. When he sings it's as much as people can do to keep from laughing. (*To* GREEN) H'are yah?[40]

'Ma', 'awfully', 'frightfully', 'don't you know', and 'H'are yah?' would be inconceivable in the language of Wilde's characters, who speak like their creator in well-formed complete sentences and rarely use slang or vogue-words. In the course of revision Wilde removed from the play a number of references to debts, traditional in the life-style of the man-about-town. The touches that identify Jack and Algernon as well-to-do bachelors are few: the consumption of champagne, the restaurant meals, the location of their apartments, and the list of alternative amusements at the end of Act I (ll. 682–92). The young women diverge from type in a similar way. Cecily is more knowing than the *ingénues* she is based on; Gwendolen is clever and independent-minded, but her fashionable elegance distinguishes her from the common image of the 'modern', intellectual woman as dowdy, straight-haired, and faddish—an image retailed in Pinero's *The Weaker Sex* and Grundy's *The New Woman* (Comedy Theatre, 1894). Miss Prism and Dr Chasuble are characterized by a few carefully-selected details: their ecclesiastical and educational enthusiasms are suggestive of the mid-century years. Chasuble's fussy precision of language is established in his first scene with Miss Prism and her pupil: even the commas are telling in 'Miss Prism, you are, I trust, well?' (II, 63–4). Wilde's revisions between the manuscript draft and the 1899 edition show that he wanted to avoid farcical exaggeration: the greater number of references to their respective preoccupations in the original version gave Miss Prism and the rector an obsessive quality. By the same process Lady Bracknell (whose name was Lady Brancaster in texts before that used by Alexander) was deprived of several lines in which the supine Lord Bracknell was mentioned.[41] Moulton the gardener originally appeared briefly in Act II (see note to ll. 1–4), but this conventionally comic rustic disappeared in the licensing copy. The remaining servants at Woolton, Merriman and the footman, are practically silent, although their presence during the tea-table scene in Act II is valuable. Lane, Algernon's butler, is anything but the confidential scheming servant of tradition—if he conforms to a type, it is a Wildean one, reminiscent of Phipps in *An Ideal Husband*: 'a mask with a manner ... He represents the dominance of form'.[42]

Sparing and strategic use of parody, and the avoidance (or

[40] A. W. Pinero, *The Weaker Sex* (1894), p. 52.

[41] See, for example, notes to II, 295 and III, 192–3.

[42] *An Ideal Husband*, p. 137/*CW*, p. 522.

GWENDOLEN AND CECILY.

GWENDOLEN : " *Well—I speak quite candidly—I wish that you were fully thirty-five, and more than usually plain for your age.*"

Irene Vanbrugh and Evelyn Millard: studio photograph by Alfred Ellis of characters in the first production.
(Reproduced from the *Sketch*, 20 March 1895)

modification) of stock characterization are complemented by restraint in the physical action of the play. There is little of the violence associated with farce—no desperate concealments or rushing in and out of doors. The struggle for the cigarette-case, the sugar and cake forced on Gwendolen, the hunt (off-stage) for the hand-bag, and Jack's search through the Army Lists are the most violent actions. The first two acts end with Jack impotently indignant and Algernon refusing to be flurried. In Act I he is complacently looking forward to a weekend's Bunburying and in Act II he is finishing his tea.

The sense of decorum in Wilde's comedy suggests the control of polite behaviour over Society. The interdependence of art, etiquette, and insincerity had been proposed in *Dorian Gray*:

> For the canons of good society are, or should be, the same as the canons of art. Form is absolutely essential to it. It should have the dignity of a ceremony, as well as its unreality, and should combine the insincere character of a romantic play with the wit and beauty that make such plays delightful to us. Is insincerity such a terrible thing? I think not. It is merely a method by which we can multiply our personalities.[43]

In *The Importance of Being Earnest* there are three major instances of etiquette in action—two afternoon calls, with tea served to the visitors, and Jack's mourning for Ernest. The manuals of etiquette devote much space to the formalities involved in the paying and receiving of calls, and death was the occasion of elaborate and carefully graduated alterations in dress and social behaviour.[44] Each of these three sequences in the play combines the practice of social forms with some kind of deception. In Act I, Lane and Algernon jointly lie about the availability of cucumbers, Jack courts Gwendolen behind her mother's back (at one point literally so), and Algernon invokes Bunbury to avoid a dinner with his aunt. Jack's behaviour, like Algernon's, is part of a general lie concerning a mythical being, in his case Ernest. In the tea-table scene in Act II the formalities of hospitality are played off against the antagonism of Gwendolen and Cecily—an antagonism that is in any case based upon misinformation deriving from the greater deceit of Bunbury and Ernest. In this sequence the sense of artifice—which has already been mentioned—is enhanced by the progression of Gwendolen from insincere and effusively proffered friendship ('My first impressions of people are never wrong'; II, 569–70) through naked hostility ('This is no time for wearing the shallow mask of manners'; II, 675–6) to genuine solidarity ('You will call

---

[43] *Dorian Gray*, ed. Murray, pp. 142–3/*CW*, p. 112. An interesting study of 'form' is Leonora Davidoff, *The Best Circles: Society Etiquette and the Season* (1973).

[44] On Victorian mourning see John Morley, *Death, Heaven and the Victorians* (1971), Chapter Six ('Mourning Dress and Etiquette').

me sister, will you not?'; II, 759)—all in fulfilment of Algernon's prophetic remark that women only call each other sister 'when they have called each other a lot of things first' (I, 675–6). As for Jack's mourning attire, which provides the play's most visually striking moment (especially if the audience sees him before the other characters do), it is a lie for which we have been well prepared without being told exactly what form it will take.[45] Cecily's indecorous exclamation—'But what horrid clothes you have got on!' (II, 296–7)—does not (as the audience knows) break the rules concerning mourning, for Ernest is not in fact dead. It does break the rules of Jack's game, and when he protests, 'What nonsense! I haven't got a brother' (II, 306), he is in the unusual position of speaking an untruth without meaning to. He means it literally, Cecily takes it figuratively ('Oh don't say that. However badly he may have behaved to you in the past he is still your brother'; II, 307–8), and within his charade it could mean that Ernest is no longer alive. The virtuous brother mourning the profligate and the unforgiving one denying his existence are figures out of some serious play, and so is the new role in which Jack is shortly to be cast—the brother forgiving a prodigal he had given up for dead. Personalities are being multiplied faster than Jack can cope with them.

It would be possible to compile an etiquette book from precepts uttered by Wilde's characters—it would include notes on the impropriety of reading a private cigarette-case and the vulgarity of arguments. A similar dossier might be provided on acceptable attitudes to political, social, and aesthetic matters, from French songs to bomb outrages. The comedy is addressed to those whose concern with life is as 'serious' as their taste in drama. Ideas that aroused enthusiasm and partisanship in the 1890s are treated not merely with flippancy but with an earnest, confident wrongness (in Gwendolen's announcement that we live in 'an age of ideals' and Lady Bracknell's remarks on education, for example). The opening conversation between Algernon and Lane establishes the manner in which serious topics will be handled. Lane is honest but alarmingly matter-of-fact about his married life:

> ... I have only been married *once*. That was in consequence of a misunderstanding between myself and a young person.

Algernon's reaction is dismissive and is spoken '*languidly*':

> I don't know that I am much interested in your family life, Lane.

Lane is not to be outdone in off-handedness:

> No, sir; it is not a very interesting subject. I never think of it myself.

[45] Wilde wisely deleted an anticipation of the effect in Act I: see note to ll. 658–9.

was specially invented for people whose memories are so   80
curiously constituted.

ALGERNON

Oh! there is no use speculating on that subject. Divorces
are made in heaven— (JACK *puts out his hand to take a
sandwich.* ALGERNON *at once interferes*) Please don't touch
the cucumber sandwiches. They are ordered specially for   85
Aunt Augusta.   *Takes one and eats it*

JACK

Well, you have been eating them all the time.

ALGERNON

That is quite a different matter. She is my aunt. (*Takes
plate from below*) Have some bread and butter. The bread
and butter is for Gwendolen. Gwendolen is devoted to   90
bread and butter.

JACK (*Advancing to table and helping himself*)

And very good bread and butter it is too.

ALGERNON

Well, my dear fellow, you need not eat as if you were going
to eat it all. You behave as if you were married to her
already. You are not married to her already, and I don't   95
think you ever will be.

JACK

Why on earth do you say that?

ALGERNON

Well, in the first place, girls never marry the men they flirt
with. Girls don't think it right.

JACK

Oh, that is nonsense!   100

ALGERNON

It isn't. It is a great truth. It accounts for the extraordinary
number of bachelors that one sees all over the place. In the
second place, I don't give my consent.

JACK

Your consent!

---

83 s.d. HTC makes the nature of the interference clear: 'ALGY *takes up plate and
puts it on his knees'.*
92 *it is too* (it looks too PR, HTC only) Altered by Wilde in proof.
102 *the place* The MS draft has the bachelors 'going about the place', which Wilde
struck out and replaced with 'that one sees all over the shop'. This slang phrase
was changed in subsequent drafts to 'all over Town'. In his alterations to WD
Wilde substituted 'the place', settling for a neutral expression.

ALGERNON

My dear fellow, Gwendolen is my first cousin. And before   105
I allow you to marry her, you will have to clear up the
whole question of Cecily.   *Rings bell*

JACK

Cecily! What on earth do you mean? What do you mean,
Algy, by Cecily? I don't know anyone of the name of
Cecily.   110

Enter LANE

ALGERNON

Bring me that cigarette case Mr Worthing left in the
smoking-room the last time he dined here.

LANE

Yes, sir.   LANE *goes out*

JACK

Do you mean to say you have had my cigarette case all this
time? I wish to goodness you had let me know. I have been   115
writing frantic letters to Scotland Yard about it. I was very
nearly offering a large reward.

ALGERNON

Well, I wish you would offer one. I happen to be more than
usually hard up.

JACK

There is no good offering a large reward now that the thing   120
is found.

Enter LANE *with the cigarette case on a salver.* ALGERNON *takes it
at once.* LANE *goes out*

105 In the MS draft Algernon refers to the country house (and its remote stables).
   If Jack marries Gwendolen, Algernon will spend the greater part of the year
   with them:
   JACK
   You certainly won't do anything of the kind, if I have anything to say in the
   matter.
   ALGERNON (*Carelessly, while taking another sandwich*) You won't, dear boy.
   Gwendolen has one of those soft yielding natures that always have their own
   way . . .
116 *Scotland Yard* In 1891 the Metropolitan Police moved to New Scotland Yard,
   on the Embankment near Westminster Bridge. Contemporary guide-books
   direct travellers to the Lost Property Office there, but Jack seems to have a
   full-scale investigation in mind.
117, 120 *a large reward* 1899, HTC (a reward PR, WD, HTC1, etc.) A happy touch
   added in proof: Alexander may be altering HTC1 to correspond with 1899.
121 s.d. Alexander's copy is helpfully explicit: '*Enter* LANE *with cigarette-case on
   salver.* ALGY *and* JACK *both try to take it.* ALGY *takes it and moves down
   R.*'

ALGERNON

I think that is rather mean of you, Ernest, I must say.
(*Opens case and examines it*) However, it makes no matter,
for, now that I look at the inscription inside, I find that the
thing isn't yours after all.   125

JACK

Of course it's mine. (*Moving to him*) You have seen me with
it a hundred times, and you have no right whatsoever to
read what is written inside. It is a very ungentlemanly
thing to read a private cigarette case.

ALGERNON

Oh! it is absurd to have a hard-and-fast rule about what one   130
should read and what one shouldn't. More than half of
modern culture depends on what one shouldn't read.

JACK

I am quite aware of the fact, and I don't propose to discuss
modern culture. It isn't the sort of thing one should talk of
in private. I simply want my cigarette case back.   135

ALGERNON

Yes; but this isn't your cigarette case. This cigarette case is
a present from someone of the name of Cecily, and you said
you didn't know anyone of that name.

JACK

Well, if you want to know, Cecily happens to be my aunt.

ALGERNON

Your aunt!   140

JACK

Yes. Charming old lady she is, too. Lives at Tunbridge
Wells. Just give it back to me, Algy.

ALGERNON (*Retreating to back of sofa*)

But why does she call herself little Cecily if she is your
aunt and lives at Tunbridge Wells? (*Reading*) 'From little
Cecily with her fondest love'.   145

---

122 *mean* 1899, HTC, MS (horrid WD, HTC1, etc.) Wilde substituted 'mean' in
    his revisions to WD.
130–5 1899, HTC1 (om. HTC only) Wilde altered the Arents I typescript, delet-
    ing 'should talk of in private' and inserting 'discuss at afternoon tea. It is a little
    too exotic', but LC reverts to the typescript's version. In the MS draft the joke
    is not as neat: 'One should read everything. That is the true basis of modern
    culture. More than half of modern culture depends on the unreadable'.
141–2 *Tunbridge Wells* An inland watering-place in Kent fashionable since the 17th
    century. An expensive resort much favoured by the upper classes.

JACK (*Moving to sofa and kneeling upon it*)

My dear fellow, what on earth is there in that? Some aunts are tall, some aunts are not tall. That is a matter that surely an aunt may be allowed to decide for herself. You seem to think that every aunt should be exactly like your aunt! That is absurd! For heaven's sake give me back my ciga-   150
rette case.   *Follows* ALGERNON *round the room*

ALGERNON

Yes. But why does your aunt call you her uncle? 'From little Cecily, with her fondest love to her dear Uncle Jack'. There is no objection, I admit, to an aunt being a small aunt, but why an aunt, no matter what her size may be,   155
should call her own nephew her uncle, I can't quite make out. Besides, your name isn't Jack at all; it is Ernest.

JACK

It isn't Ernest; it's Jack.

ALGERNON

You have always told me it was Ernest. I have introduced you to everyone as Ernest. You answer to the name of   160
Ernest. You look as if your name was Ernest. You are the most earnest looking person I ever saw in my life. It is perfectly absurd your saying that your name isn't Ernest. It's on your cards. Here is one of them (*Taking it from case*) 'Mr Ernest Worthing, B.4, The Albany'. I'll keep this as a   165
proof that your name is Ernest if ever you attempt to deny it to me, or to Gwendolen, or to anyone else.

Puts the card in his pocket

JACK

Well, my name is Ernest in town and Jack in the country, and the cigarette case was given to me in the country.

ALGERNON

Yes, but that does not account for the fact that your small   170
Aunt Cecily, who lives at Tunbridge Wells, calls you her dear uncle. Come, old boy, you had much better have the thing out at once.

JACK

My dear Algy, you talk exactly as if you were a dentist. It is

---

151 s.d. In 1899 Algernon is misnamed 'Ernest' here: Ross's edition corrects the mistake.
165 See Appendix IV, p. 117.

very vulgar to talk like a dentist when one isn't a dentist. It   175
produces a false impression.

ALGERNON

Well, that is exactly what dentists always do. Now, go on!
Tell me the whole thing. I may mention that I have always
suspected you of being a confirmed and secret Bunburyist;
and I am quite sure of it now.   180

JACK

Bunburyist? What on earth do you mean by a Bunburyist?

ALGERNON

I'll reveal to you the meaning of that incomparable expression as soon as you are kind enough to inform me why you
are Ernest in town and Jack in the country.

JACK

Well, produce my cigarette case first.   185

ALGERNON

Here it is. (*Hands cigarette case*) Now produce your explanation, and pray make it improbable.   *Sits on sofa*

JACK

My dear fellow, there is nothing improbable about my
explanation at all. In fact it's perfectly ordinary. Old Mr
Thomas Cardew, who adopted me when I was a little boy,   190
made me in his will guardian to his grand-daughter, Miss
Cecily Cardew. Cecily, who addresses me as her uncle

---

186 Alexander's notes show that Algernon takes a cigarette from the case before
handing it over, and Jack takes one before he puts it in his pocket. They light
their cigarettes at ll. 202 and 213, respectively. Cigarettes (preferably gold-
tipped) were a favourite Wildean prop, in both life and works. Cf. *Dorian Gray*,
where Lord Henry insists that the painter Basil Hallward smoke one: '. . . I
can't allow you to smoke cigars. You must have a cigarette. A cigarette is the
perfect type of a perfect pleasure. It is exquisite, and it leaves one unsatisfied.
What more can one want?' (ed. Murray, p. 84/*CW*, p. 70).

187 *improbable* (remarkable HTC1, etc.) Alexander deletes the whole phrase,
ending Algernon's speech with 'explanation'. He retains the s.d. '*sits on sofa*',
cuts the first two sentences of Jack's reply, and lets a further s.d. '*sits C.*'
remain. After the struggle for the cigarette-case this creates stillness and
concentration on stage for the vital information that Jack is an adopted child
and Cecily's guardian. In LC Algernon's speech continues after 'remarkable':
'The bore about most explanations is that they are never half so remarkable as
the things they try to explain, that is why modern science is so absolutely
tedious'.

188–9 *My dear fellow . . . ordinary* (om. HTC only) HTC1 and earlier versions read
'remarkable' for 'improbable'.

from motives of respect that you could not possibly appreciate, lives at my place in the country under the charge of her admirable governess, Miss Prism.   195

ALGERNON

Where is that place in the country, by the way?

JACK

That is nothing to you, dear boy. You are not going to be invited—I may tell you candidly that the place is not in Shropshire.

ALGERNON

I suspected that, my dear fellow! I have Bunburyed all   200
over Shropshire on two separate occasions. Now, go on. Why are you Ernest in town and Jack in the country?

JACK

My dear Algy, I don't know whether you will be able to understand my real motives. You are hardly serious enough. When one is placed in the position of guardian,   205
one has to adopt a very high moral tone on all subjects. It's one's duty to do so. And as a high moral tone can hardly be said to conduce very much to either one's health or one's happiness, in order to get up to town I have always pretended to have a younger brother of the name of Ernest,   210
who lives in the Albany, and gets into the most dreadful scrapes. That, my dear Algy, is the whole truth pure and simple.

ALGERNON

The truth is rarely pure and never simple. Modern life would be very tedious if it were either, and modern litera-   215
ture a complete impossibility!

JACK

That wouldn't be at all a bad thing.

ALGERNON

Literary criticism is not your forte my dear fellow. Don't try it. You should leave that to people who haven't been at a University. They do it so well in the daily papers. What   220

193–4 *that ... appreciate* 1899, HTC (om. HTC1, etc.)
203–5 *I don't know ... enough* 1899, HTC1, etc. (om. HTC only)
214–20 See Appendix IV, pp. 117–18.

you really are is a Bunburyist. I was quite right in saying you were a Bunburyist. You are one of the most advanced Bunburyists I know.

JACK

What on earth do you mean?

ALGERNON

You have invented a very useful younger brother called   225
Ernest, in order that you may be able to come up to town as often as you like. I have invented an invaluable permanent invalid called Bunbury, in order that I may be able to go down into the country whenever I choose. Bunbury is perfectly invaluable. If it wasn't for Bunbury's extra-   230
ordinary bad health, for instance, I wouldn't be able to dine with you at Willis's to-night, for I have been really engaged to Aunt Augusta for more than a week.

JACK

I haven't asked you to dine with me anywhere to-night.

ALGERNON

I know. You are absurdly careless about sending out invi-   235
tations. It is very foolish of you. Nothing annoys people so much as not receiving invitations.

JACK

You had much better dine with your Aunt Augusta.

ALGERNON

I haven't the smallest intention of doing anything of the kind. To begin with, I dined there on Monday, and once a   240
week is quite enough to dine with one's own relations. In the second place, whenever I do dine there I am always treated as a member of the family, and sent down with either no woman at all, or two. In the third place, I know perfectly well whom she will place me next to, to-night.   245

221–2 *I was quite right ... Bunburyist* 1899, HTC1, etc. (om. HTC only)
232 *Willis's* 1899, WD, HTC1, MS (the Savoy HTC, LC, etc.) Willis's was a fashionable restaurant in King Street, near the St James's Theatre: like the Savoy Hotel in the Strand it was much frequented by Wilde. In the MS draft of Act II an attempt is made to arrest Algernon for a debt to the Savoy (see Appendix I) and in LC 'Nothing annoys people so much as not receiving invitations' is followed by a four-speech exchange in which Jack admits to owing the hotel £120—he could afford to settle up, but feels he must maintain Ernest's reputation as 'one of those chaps who never pay a bill'.
239 In HTC Algernon makes himself comfortable for this speech: he '*crosses to sofa, R., takes cushion from lower end, puts it against the one at upper end*' and then '*Sits upper end, puts feet up, head on cushions*'.
241–4 Guests assembled upstairs in the drawing-room before dinner, and each gentleman was appointed escort to a lady for the evening—he was 'sent down' to the dining-room with her.

She will place me next Mary Farquhar, who always flirts
with her own husband across the dinner-table. That is not
very pleasant. Indeed, it is not even decent—and that sort
of thing is enormously on the increase. The amount of
women in London who flirt with their own husbands is   250
perfectly scandalous. It looks so bad. It is simply washing
one's clean linen in public. Besides, now that I know you to
be a confirmed Bunburyist I naturally want to talk to you
about Bunburying. I want to tell you the rules.

JACK

I'm not a Bunburyist at all. If Gwendolen accepts me, I am   255
going to kill my brother, indeed I think I'll kill him in any
case. Cecily is a little too much interested in him. It is
rather a bore. So I am going to get rid of Ernest. And I
strongly advise you to do the same with Mr—with your
invalid friend who has the absurd name.   260

ALGERNON

Nothing will induce me to part with Bunbury, and if you
ever get married, which seems to me extremely problema-
tic, you will be very glad to know Bunbury. A man who
marries without knowing Bunbury has a very tedious time
of it.   265

JACK

That is nonsense. If I marry a charming girl like
Gwendolen, and she is the only girl I ever saw in my life
that I would marry, I certainly won't want to know Bunbury.

ALGERNON

Then your wife will. You don't seem to realize, that in   270
married life three is company and two is none.

JACK (*Sententiously*)

That, my dear young friend, is the theory that the corrupt
French Drama has been propounding for the last fifty years.

246–52 Cf. the less sophisticated joke in *Lady Windermere's Fan*: 'It's most dangerous nowadays for a husband to pay any attention to his wife in public. It always
makes people think that he beats her when they're alone. The world has grown
suspicious of anything that looks like a happy married life' (p. 63 /*CW*, p. 400).

263 *you will be very glad to know Bunbury* Cf. Lord Henry Wotton in *Dorian Gray*:
'. . . the one charm of marriage is that it makes a life of deception absolutely
necessary for both parties' (ed. Murray, p. 4/*CW*, p. 20).

272–3 *the corrupt French Drama* The plays of Dumas *fils*, Scribe, Augier, and
others were enormously popular and influential in Britain, but considerable
alteration was necessary to suit them to British attitudes: their treatment of
sexual misconduct was considered far too liberal and frank.

ALGERNON

Yes; and that the happy English home has proved in half
the time. 275

JACK

For heaven's sake, don't try to be cynical. It's perfectly
easy to be cynical.

ALGERNON

My dear fellow, it isn't easy to be anything nowadays.
There's such a lot of beastly competition about. (*The sound
of an electric bell is heard*) Ah! that must be Aunt Augusta. 280
Only relatives, or creditors, ever ring in that Wagnerian
manner. Now, if I get her out of the way for ten minutes,
so that you can have an opportunity for proposing to
Gwendolen, may I dine with you to-night at Willis's?

JACK

I suppose so, if you want to. 285

ALGERNON

Yes, but you must be serious about it. I hate people who
are not serious about meals. It is so shallow of them.

Enter LANE

276 Texts before HTC and 1899 have a different version of the conversation after l.
275. Algy continues (in the MS draft):

That is the worst of the English. They are always degrading truths into facts,
and when truths become facts they lose all their intellectual value.

JACK

Do you always really understand what you say, Algy?

ALGERNON (*After consideration*)

Yes—if I listen attentively.

JACK

Then you have certainly more brains than I have ever given you credit for.

ALGERNON

My dear fellow, until you believe that I have got absolute genius there will
always be a slight coldness between us. (*A ring*) . . .

281 *Wagnerian* (argumentative PR) The sentence was added to WD and revised in
proof. The operas of Richard Wagner, especially *Tristan und Isolde* and *Tann-
häuser*, were much favoured by the *avant-garde*, but Wilde was quite happy to
use the popular joke of the loudness of the music. In *Dorian Gray* Lady Henry
Wotton professes to like Wagnerian opera best: 'It is so loud that one can talk
the whole time without other people hearing what one says. That is a great
advantage . . .' (ed. Murray, p. 45/*CW*, p. 47).

284 *Willis's* Changed to 'the Savoy' by Alexander to agree with his earlier reference.

LANE

Lady Bracknell and Miss Fairfax.

ALGERNON *goes forward to meet them. Enter* LADY BRACKNELL
and GWENDOLEN

LADY BRACKNELL

Good afternoon, dear Algernon, I hope you are behaving
very well. 290

ALGERNON

I'm feeling very well, Aunt Augusta.

LADY BRACKNELL

That's not quite the same thing. In fact the two things
rarely go together.
Sees JACK *and bows to him with icy coldness*

ALGERNON (*To* GWENDOLEN)

Dear me, you are smart!

GWENDOLEN

I am always smart! Aren't I, Mr Worthing? 295

JACK

You're quite perfect, Miss Fairfax.

GWENDOLEN

Oh! I hope I am not that. It would leave no room for
developments, and I intend to develop in many directions.
GWENDOLEN *and* JACK *sit down together in the corner*

---

289 *Good afternoon, dear Algernon* (Well, dear Algernon HTC, LC, MS) The
alteration (to WD) probably reflects the repetitions of 'well' in the lines
following.

289–90 *behaving very well* 1899 (behaving well, PR, HTC, etc.)

291 *very well* 1899 (well PR, HTC; quite well LC, Arents I)

292–3 *In fact ... together* 1899, HTC (om. HTC1, etc.) The s.d. following ('*Bows
distantly to* JACK') was added to WD to replace a greeting ('Good afternoon, Mr
Worthing') There is no MS equivalent of ll. 290–3: this intensive reworking of
details reflects the anxiety to make Lady Bracknell's first words effective.

295 The MS draft includes a brief exchange between Algernon and Gwendolen on
her smartness (being clever may not suit others, but it is 'excessively becoming'
to her) and a reference by Lady Brancaster to Algernon's debts): 'Of course I
never mention anything about them to your uncle. Indeed, as you know, I
never mention anything to him at all'. Like a number of other references to
debts and Lord Bracknell, these were removed at an early stage in revision.

297–8 The speech was added to WD. In Alexander's copy Jack and Gwendolen '*go
up to fireplace*' at this point.

LADY BRACKNELL

I'm sorry if we are a little late, Algernon, but I was obliged
to call on dear Lady Harbury. I hadn't been there since her   300
poor husband's death. I never saw a woman so altered; she
looks quite twenty years younger. And now I'll have a cup
of tea, and one of those nice cucumber sandwiches you
promised me.

ALGERNON

Certainly, Aunt Augusta.   *Goes over to tea table* 305

LADY BRACKNELL

Won't you come and sit here, Gwendolen?

GWENDOLEN

Thanks, mamma, I'm quite comfortable where I am.

ALGERNON (*Picking up empty plate in horror*)

Good heavens! Lane! Why are there no cucumber sandwiches? I ordered them specially.

LANE (*Gravely*)

There were no cucumbers in the market this morning, sir.   310
I went down twice.

ALGERNON

No cucumbers!

LANE

No, sir. Not even for ready money.

ALGERNON

That will do, Lane, thank you.

LANE

Thank you, sir.   *Goes out* 315

ALGERNON

I am greatly distressed, Aunt Augusta, about there being
no cucumbers, not even for ready money.

299–304 After the first sentence of this speech Alexander has Lane enter with a
tea-pot and pour a cup for Lady Bracknell (milk is added later by Algernon).
Among published texts, only the two French's editions provide this s.d., which
is necessary if the tea is to be drinkable (which it will not be if the pot has been
on stage since the opening of the act).

312–15 *No cucumbers! . . . Thank you, sir.* 1899, HTC (om. HTC1, etc.) Added to
WD.

316 *I am . . . there being* (I'm greatly distressed, Aunt Augusta, there were HTC;
om. HTC1, etc.) Added by Wilde to the WD typescript, ll. 312–17 are not
found before HTC1.

LADY BRACKNELL

It really makes no matter, Algernon. I had some crumpets
with Lady Harbury, who seems to me to be living entirely
for pleasure now.   320

ALGERNON

I hear her hair has turned quite gold from grief.

LADY BRACKNELL

It certainly has changed its colour. From what cause I, of
course, cannot say. (ALGERNON *crosses and hands tea*)
Thank you. I've quite a treat for you to-night, Algernon. I
am going to send you down with Mary Farquhar. She is   325
such a nice woman, and so attentive to her husband. It's
delightful to watch them.

ALGERNON

I am afraid, Aunt Augusta, I shall have to give up the
pleasure of dining with you to-night after all.

LADY BRACKNELL (*Frowning*)

I hope not, Algernon. It would put my table completely   330
out. Your uncle would have to dine upstairs. Fortunately
he is accustomed to that.

ALGERNON

It is a great bore, and, I need hardly say, a terrible disappointment to me, but the fact is I have just had a
telegram to say that my poor friend Bunbury is very ill   335
again. (*Exchanges glances with* JACK) They seem to think I
should be with him.

LADY BRACKNELL

It is very strange. This Mr Bunbury seems to suffer from
curiously bad health.

ALGERNON

Yes; poor Bunbury is a dreadful invalid.   340

LADY BRACKNELL

Well, I must say, Algernon, that I think it is high time that
Mr Bunbury made up his mind whether he was going to
live or to die. This shilly-shallying with the question is
absurd. Nor do I in any way approve of the modern
sympathy with invalids. I consider it morbid. Illness of   345

---

321 *quite gold from grief* Cf. Lord Henry Wotton's description of Mme de Ferrol, in
      Dorian Gray: 'Her capacity for family affection is extraordinary. When her
      third husband died, her hair turned quite gold from grief' (ed. Murray, p.
      178/*CW*, p. 136).

322 Alexander has Gwendolen and Jack come to the tea-table on this line: she '*pours
      out two cups, they both drink and talk*'.

333–4 *and . . . to me* (om. HTC, etc.) Added to WD.

344–5 *the modern . . . invalids* Cf. Introduction, pp. xxxiii–iv.

any kind is hardly a thing to be encouraged in others.
Health is the primary duty of life. I am always telling that
to your poor uncle, but he never seems to take much
notice—as far as any improvement in his ailments goes. I
should be much obliged if you would ask Mr Bunbury,   350
from me, to be kind enough not to have a relapse on
Saturday, for I rely on you to arrange my music for me. It
is my last reception, and one wants something that will
encourage conversation, particularly at the end of the
season when everyone has practically said whatever they   355
had to say, which, in most cases, was probably not much.

ALGERNON

I'll speak to Bunbury, Aunt Augusta, if he is still conscious, and I think I can promise you he'll be all right by
Saturday. Of course the music is a great difficulty. You
see, if one plays good music, people don't listen, and if one   360
plays bad music people don't talk. But I'll run over the
programme I've drawn out, if you will kindly come into the
next room for a moment.

LADY BRACKNELL

Thank you, Algernon. It is very thoughtful of you.
(*Rising, and following* ALGERNON) I'm sure the programme   365
will be delightful, after a few expurgations. French songs I
cannot possibly allow. People always seem to think that
they are improper, and either look shocked, which is vulgar, or laugh, which is worse. But German sounds a
thoroughly respectable language, and indeed, I believe is   370
so. Gwendolen, you will accompany me.

356 *which ... not much* (om. HTC, etc.) Added to WD.

357–8 *if he is still conscious* 1899, HTC (om. HTC1, etc.) Added to WD.

361 *people don't talk* The joke of musicians invited to play at receptions and annoyed
  to find their music drowned by conversation occurs frequently in *Punch*
  cartoons of the 1880s and 1890s. In the MS draft Wilde includes references to
  Gwendolen's cleverness (Algernon cannot discuss music with her—'She has
  grown far too intellectual ... She seems to think that music does not contain
  enough useful information')—and to the University Extension Scheme (see
  III, 76–82 and Appendix IV, p. 125).

366–71 *French songs ... I believe is so* (om. HTC, LC) Added to WD. Arents I has a
  manuscript revision derived from a passage in the MS draft, but not adopted in
  either of its forms: 'You see, I should like your uncle to be able to be present, as
  most of the music of our day discusses every modern topic far too openly:
  especially orchestral music. A little more reticence would be an advantage'.

GWENDOLEN

Certainly, mamma.

LADY BRACKNELL *and* ALGERNON *go into the music-room.*
GWENDOLEN *remains behind*

JACK

Charming day it has been, Miss Fairfax.

GWENDOLEN

Pray don't talk to me about the weather, Mr Worthing.
Whenever people talk to me about the weather, I always   375
feel quite certain that they mean something else. And that
makes me so nervous.

JACK

I do mean something else.

GWENDOLEN

I thought so. In fact, I am never wrong.

JACK

And I would like to be allowed to take advantage of Lady   380
Bracknell's temporary absence—

GWENDOLEN

I would certainly advise you to do so. Mamma has a way of
coming back suddenly into a room that I have often had to
speak to her about.

JACK (*Nervously*)

Miss Fairfax, ever since I met you I have admired you   385
more than any girl—I have ever met since—I met you.

GWENDOLEN

Yes, I am quite aware of the fact. And I often wish that in
public, at any rate, you had been more demonstrative. For
me you have always had an irresistible fascination. Even
before I met you I was far from indifferent to you. (JACK   390
looks at her in amazement) We live, as I hope you know, Mr

374 Alexander's s.d. suggests a certain matter-of-fact assurance in Gwendolen's
manner: she '*comes down right, throws wrap over back of sofa then sits down-stage*'.
379 *In fact ... wrong* 1899 (om. HTC, etc.) Added to WD.
386 The pauses in this line are added to WD. In Arents I the first 'met' and the final
'you' are underlined—if the line is spoken quickly and stressed in the way this
indicates, the comic effect produced is less sympathetic than the hesitation
indicated by the dashes.

Worthing, in an age of ideals. The fact is constantly mentioned in the more expensive monthly magazines, and has reached the provincial pulpits I am told: and my ideal has always been to love some one of the name of Ernest. There   395 is something in that name that inspires absolute confidence. The moment Algernon first mentioned to me that he had a friend called Ernest, I knew I was destined to love you.

JACK

You really love me, Gwendolen?   400

GWENDOLEN

Passionately!

JACK

Darling! You don't know how happy you've made me.

GWENDOLEN

My own Ernest!

JACK

But you don't mean to say that you couldn't love me if my name wasn't Ernest?   405

GWENDOLEN

But your name is Ernest.

JACK

Yes, I know it is. But supposing it was something else? Do you mean to say you couldn't love me then?

GWENDOLEN (*Glibly*)

Ah! that is clearly a metaphysical speculation, and like most metaphysical speculations has very little reference at   410 all to the actual facts of real life, as we know them.

JACK

Personally, darling, to speak quite candidly, I don't much care about the name of Ernest—I don't think the name suits me at all.

393–4 *and has reached . . . I am told* 1899, HTC (om. HTC1, etc.) Added to WD. There is no equivalent in the MS draft for the whole sentence. Given Wilde's views on the press, the implication that provincial pulpits are the ultimate stage in the progress of popular ethics through the media is particularly barbed. Cf. Dr Chasuble's preaching, as hinted at in II, 240–51 and III, 310–12.

400 *You really love me, Gwendolen?* Jack uses her Christian name for the first time, an intimacy appropriate only between close relatives and those married or engaged to be married. The conversation becomes more intimate (in Alexander's s.d. she '*puts arms around* JACK'*s neck*' at l. 401) until Jack mentions marriage, and Gwendolen reminds him that an essential formality has been left out by reverting to 'Mr Worthing'.

410 *most* (all PR, HTC, etc.) Altered in proof.

GWENDOLEN

It suits you perfectly. It is a divine name. It has a music of   415
its own. It produces vibrations.

JACK

Well, really, Gwendolen, I must say that I think there are
lots of other much nicer names. I think Jack, for instance, a
charming name.

GWENDOLEN

Jack?—No, there is very little music in the name Jack, if   420
any at all, indeed. It does not thrill. It produces absolutely
no vibrations—I have known several Jacks, and they all,
without exception, were more than usually plain. Besides,
Jack is a notorious domesticity for John! And I pity any
woman who is married to a man called John. She would   425
probably never be allowed to know the entrancing pleasure
of a single moment's solitude. The only really safe name is
Ernest.

JACK

Gwendolen, I must get christened at once—I mean we
must get married at once. There is no time to be lost.   430

GWENDOLEN

Married, Mr Worthing?

JACK (*Astounded*)

Well—surely. You know that I love you, and you led me to
believe, Miss Fairfax, that you were not absolutely indifferent to me.

GWENDOLEN

I adore you. But you haven't proposed to me yet. Nothing   435
has been said at all about marriage. The subject has not
even been touched on.

JACK

Well—may I propose to you now?

GWENDOLEN

I think it would be an admirable opportunity. And to spare
you any possible disappointment, Mr Worthing, I think it   440
only fair to tell you quite frankly beforehand that I am fully
determined to accept you.

420 *Jack?* Alexander adds a repetition of the name, with three exclamation marks.
435 *I adore you* In Alexander's s.d. she '*puts hands on* JACK'*s shoulders for a moment*'.

JACK

Gwendolen!

GWENDOLEN

Yes, Mr Worthing, what have you got to say to me?

JACK

You know what I have got to say to you. 445

GWENDOLEN

Yes, but you don't say it.

JACK

Gwendolen, will you marry me?   *Goes on his knees*

GWENDOLEN

Of course I will, darling. How long you have been about it!
I am afraid you have had very little experience in how to
propose. 450

JACK

My own one, I have never loved anyone in the world but
you.

GWENDOLEN

Yes, but men often propose for practice. I know my
brother Gerald does. All my girl-friends tell me so. What
wonderfully blue eyes you have, Ernest! They are quite, 455
quite, blue. I hope you will always look at me just like that,
especially when there are other people present.

Enter LADY BRACKNELL

LADY BRACKNELL

Mr Worthing! Rise, sir, from this semi-recumbent post-
ure. It is most indecorous.

GWENDOLEN

Mamma! (*He tries to rise; she restrains him*) I must beg you 460

443–6 *Gwendolen! . . . say it* 1899, HTC1, etc. (om. HTC only)
447 Alexander alters this to 'Then, Gwendolen, you will marry me?'
454 *All my girl-friends tell me so* 1899, HTC (He tells me so PR, HTC1, etc.)
458–9 Alexander emphasizes the way in which Gwendolen takes the initiative.
    Lady Bracknell repeats her exclamation, 'Mr Worthing!', but when Jack tries
    to stand up, Gwendolen '*pushes him down with her hands on his shoulders*',
    business repeated after Gwendolen's first reply to her mother. When she
    announces the engagement, Gwendolen rises and '*lifts* JACK *up by placing her
    hand underneath his elbows*'. In the MS draft Lady Brancaster asks whether it is
    the 'modern idea' that 'the engagement should come first, and the proposal
    afterwards'.

to retire. This is no place for you. Besides, Mr Worthing
has not quite finished yet.

LADY BRACKNELL

Finished what, may I ask?

GWENDOLEN

I am engaged to Mr Worthing, mamma. *They rise together*

LADY BRACKNELL

Pardon me, you are not engaged to anyone. When you do   465
become engaged to some one, I, or your father, should his
health permit him, will inform you of the fact. An engagement should come on a young girl as a surprise, pleasant or
unpleasant, as the case may be. It is hardly a matter that
she could be allowed to arrange for herself—And now I   470
have a few questions to put to you, Mr Worthing. While I
am making these inquiries, you, Gwendolen, will wait for
me below in the carriage.

GWENDOLEN (*Reproachfully*)

Mamma!

LADY BRACKNELL

In the carriage, Gwendolen! (GWENDOLEN *goes to the*   475
door. She and JACK *blow kisses to each other behind* LADY
BRACKNELL'*s back.* LADY BRACKNELL *looks vaguely about as if
she could not understand what the noise was. Finally turns
round*) Gwendolen, the carriage!

GWENDOLEN

Yes, mamma.   *Goes out, looking back at* JACK

LADY BRACKNELL (*Sitting down*)

You can take a seat, Mr Worthing.

                    Looks in her pocket for note-book and pencil

JACK

Thank you, Lady Bracknell, I prefer standing.

---

468 *pleasant* In Alexander's copy Lady Bracknell '*stares at* JACK, *then goes L. a little,
     turns*', after this word, making it quite evident which sort of surprise she
     considers the present one to be.

475 s.d. Alexander's alterations to this business suggest that Jack kissed Gwendo-
     len's hand, and that the blowing of kisses to one another may have been
     omitted.

479 The MS draft has stage-business here not adopted in any subsequent version:
     '*Pulls out cigarette case from his pocket and opens it.* LADY BRANCASTER *glares at
     him. He looks ashamed and replaces it quietly in his pocket*'. This may have been
     dropped on the grounds that it would be unmannerly (and therefore uncharac-
     teristic) of Jack to smoke in the presence of a lady.

LADY BRACKNELL (*Pencil and note-book in hand*)

I feel bound to tell you that you are not down on my list of   480
eligible young men, although I have the same list as the
dear Duchess of Bolton has. We work together, in fact.
However, I am quite ready to enter your name, should
your answers be what a really affectionate mother requires.
Do you smoke?   485

JACK

Well, yes, I must admit I smoke.

LADY BRACKNELL

I am glad to hear it. A man should always have an occupation of some kind. There are far too many idle men in
London as it is. How old are you?

JACK

Twenty-nine.   490

LADY BRACKNELL

A very good age to be married at. I have always been of
opinion that a man who desires to get married should know
either everything or nothing. Which do you know?

JACK (*After some hesitation*)

I know nothing, Lady Bracknell.

LADY BRACKNELL

I am pleased to hear it. I do not approve of anything that   495
tampers with natural ignorance. Ignorance is like a delicate
exotic fruit; touch it and the bloom is gone. The whole
theory of modern education is radically unsound. Fortunately in England, at any rate, education produces no
effect whatsoever. If it did, it would prove a serious danger   500
to the upper classes, and probably lead to acts of violence in
Grosvenor Square. What is your income?

---

490 *Twenty-nine* Jack's age in 1899, HTC1, LC, and Arents I. (The MS draft has
twenty-five.) Alexander altered HTC1 to thirty-five—he was thirty-six himself when the play was first performed.

493 *either everything or nothing* Cf. *Dorian Gray*, where Lord Henry Wotton com-
forts Dorian after the hero has realized that Sybil Vane, the actress he loves, is
without talent: 'She is very lovely, and if she knows as little about life as she
does about acting, she will be a delightful experience. There are only two kinds
of people who are really fascinating—people who know absolutely everything,
and people who know absolutely nothing' (ed. Murray, p. 84/*CW*, p. 73).

495 *I am pleased to hear it* Alexander has Jack sit down at this point.

500–2 *If it did ... in Grosvenor Square* 1899, HTC (om. HTC1, etc.). In proof
Wilde added the final three words, with their dark suggestion of an uprising in
the fashionable districts.

JACK

Between seven and eight thousand a year.

LADY BRACKNELL (*Makes a note in her book*)

In land, or in investments?

JACK

In investments, chiefly.　　　　　　　　　　　　　　　505

LADY BRACKNELL

That is satisfactory. What between the duties expected of
one during one's lifetime, and the duties exacted from one
after one's death, land has ceased to be either a profit or a
pleasure. It gives one position, and prevents one from
keeping it up. That's all that can be said about land.　　510

JACK

I have a country house with some land, of course, attached
to it, about fifteen hundred acres, I believe; but I don't
depend on that for my real income. In fact, as far as I can
make out, the poachers are the only people who make
anything out of it.　　　　　　　　　　　　　　　　515

LADY BRACKNELL

A country house! How many bedrooms? Well, that point can
be cleared up afterwards. You have a town house, I hope? A
girl with a simple, unspoiled nature, like Gwendolen, could
hardly be expected to reside in the country.

---

503 *Between seven ... year* Quite a fortune, at a time when a working man was lucky
if he was paid 20 shillings a week and £1,000 a year 'represented considerable
worldly success, though not great wealth, and placed a man, economically
speaking, well towards the top of the middle classes' (W. J. Reader, *Professional
Men: the Rise of the Professional Classes in Nineteenth-Century England*, 1962, p.
202). F. M. L. Thompson (*English Landed Society in the Nineteenth Century*,
1963), reckoning income at a pound per annum per acre, considers £10,000 a
year as a high level among the landowning class, exceeded only by the income of
the great magnates.

510 *land* 1899, HTC (it HTC1, etc.) The MS draft of this pronouncement is less
elegantly expressed: 'Land, nowadays, is simply a question of life-duties and
death-duties. Both of them intolerable'. The 1894 budget had consolidated the
death-duties on inherited estates, a measure hardly calculated to please Lady
Bracknell. She shares the anxieties of her class in what Thompson calls their
'Indian Summer' of influence. He quotes (p. 315) a private letter from a Kent
landowner to a neighbour in the 1890s: 'Land is no longer an enviable possession unless it is coupled with a good income from other sources'.

513–15 *In fact ... out of it* (om. HTC, etc.) Added to WD.

JACK

Well, I own a house in Belgrave Square, but it is let by the   520
year to Lady Bloxham. Of course, I can get it back
whenever I like, at six months' notice.

LADY BRACKNELL

Lady Bloxham? I don't know her.

JACK

Oh, she goes about very little. She is a lady considerably
advanced in years.   525

LADY BRACKNELL

Ah, nowadays that is no guarantee of respectability of
character. What number in Belgrave Square?

JACK

149.

LADY BRACKNELL (*Shaking her head*)

The unfashionable side. I thought there was something.
However, that could easily be altered.   530

JACK

Do you mean the fashion, or the side?

LADY BRACKNELL (*Sternly*)

Both, if necessary, I presume. What are your politics?

JACK

Well, I am afraid I really have none. I am a Liberal
Unionist.

521–9 *Bloxham* is a village in Oxfordshire, but Wilde may have recalled John
Francis Bloxam, editor of *The Chameleon*, in which his 'Phrases and
Philosophies for the Use of the Young' appeared in December 1894. In the MS
draft Lady Brancaster consults a red book before pronouncing on the status of
number 149 (in fact there were only forty-nine numbers in the square) and
adds: 'But I do not wish to seem in any way to speak slightingly of Belgrave
Square—There is far too little reverence shown, nowadays, as it is, for the few
places left to us in England that are of any social importance. I merely
mentioned that the side was not the fashionable side. But that could be altered'.
HTC follows earlier texts in adding Lady Bracknell's name at the end of Jack's
query (l. 531).

533–4 *a Liberal Unionist* Strictly speaking, Liberal Unionists were originally members of Gladstone's Liberal Party who voted against his 1886 bill for Home
Rule in Ireland, but Jack uses the term as if it were the equivalent of 'don't
know'. Wilde evidently wanted some kind of political joke, but could not at first
decide on its form. In the MS draft Jack is asked if he has any sympathy with
the Radicals and replies: 'Oh, I don't want to pit [?put] the asses against the
classes, if that is what you mean, Lady Brancaster'. To the Arents I typescript
Wilde added an additional line—'the difficulty is to find out which side the
asses are'—but this was not adopted in LC. After LC the joke disappeared,
perhaps because a reference to Radicalism added at l. 542 made it redundant.

LADY BRACKNELL

Oh, they count as Tories. They dine with us. Or come in   535
the evening, at any rate. Now to minor matters. Are your
parents living?

JACK

I have lost both my parents.

LADY BRACKNELL

Both? To lose one parent may be regarded as a misfortune
—to lose *both* seems like carelessness. Who was your   540
father? He was evidently a man of some wealth. Was he
born in what the Radical papers call the purple of com-
merce, or did he rise from the ranks of the aristocracy?

JACK

I am afraid I really don't know. The fact is, Lady
Bracknell, I said I had lost my parents. It would be   545
nearer the truth to say that my parents seem to have lost
me—I don't actually know who I am by birth. I
was—well, I was found.

LADY BRACKNELL

Found!

JACK

The late Mr Thomas Cardew, an old gentleman of a very   550
charitable and kindly disposition, found me, and gave me
the name of Worthing, because he happened to have a
first-class ticket for Worthing in his pocket at the time.
Worthing is a place in Sussex. It is a seaside resort.

539–40 *Both? To lose one parent may be regarded as a misfortune—to lose* both *seems like*
carelessness HTC (Both?—that seems like carelessness 1899) Wilde made this
alteration in WD, but Ross gives a longer version ('To lose one parent, Mr
Worthing, may be regarded as a misfortune; to lose both looks like carelessness') which has become current and which actresses and readers may prefer.
The present edition defies the author's final decision, reverting to the line as it
appears in texts before WD: the authority for the precise form of Ross's reading
is not apparent.

541 *was evidently* (seems to have been HTC) LC and earlier versions read simply
'Who was your father? A country gentleman?' and omit the final sentence of the
speech.

542 *what the radical papers call* 1899, HTC (what we must call nowadays PR)
Changed by Wilde in proof: Alexander seems to be following 1899 in adding
this phrase to HTC1. The transfer of power from the landed aristocracy to
those who had acquired wealth through trade was accompanied in the period
1880–1914 by what Thompson calls a 'partial but definite transformation of the
titled upper class' through the creation of new peerages.

554 The two concluding sentences of the speech are omitted by Alexander.

LADY BRACKNELL

Where did the charitable gentleman who had a first-class   555
ticket for this seaside resort find you?

JACK (*Gravely*)

In a hand-bag.

LADY BRACKNELL

A hand-bag?

JACK (*Very seriously*)

Yes, Lady Bracknell. I was in a hand-bag—a somewhat
large, black leather hand-bag, with handles to it—an ordi-   560
nary hand-bag in fact.

LADY BRACKNELL

In what locality did this Mr James, or Thomas, Cardew
come across this ordinary hand-bag?

JACK

In the cloak-room at Victoria Station. It was given to him
in mistake for his own.   565

LADY BRACKNELL

The cloak-room at Victoria Station?

JACK

Yes. The Brighton line.

LADY BRACKNELL

The line is immaterial. Mr Worthing, I confess I feel
somewhat bewildered by what you have just told me. To
be born, or at any rate bred, in a hand-bag, whether it had   570
handles or not, seems to me to display a contempt for the
ordinary decencies of family life that reminds one of the

---

556 *this seaside resort* 1899, HTC1 (Worthing HTC; the seaside resort, LC, Arents
I, OCT) There is no equivalent for the line in the MS draft.

562 *In what locality . . . Cardew* 1899, Arents I. The proof (PR) and HTC1 omit 'or
Thomas' which Wilde added to WD: LC reads simply 'In what locality did Mr
Cardew' and the MS draft 'Where did Mr Cardew'. (Alexander adds 'particular' before 'locality'.) It is hard to see the significance of Lady Bracknell's
uncertainty (unless she is above remembering the first names of unimportant
people?). Wilde and Alexander obviously thought the point worth pursuing.

566–7 (om. HTC) In PR, HTC1, and earlier texts the lines are included and Jack
replies 'Yes, Brighton line'. The *cloak-room* is the left-luggage office. Victoria
was the terminus for two railway companies, the London, Brighton and South
Coast Railway and the London, Chatham and Dover Railway: they had
separate but adjoining facilities.

568 *The line is immaterial* 1899, HTC1, etc. (om. HTC only) Alexander has Lady
Bracknell *'rise'* on this line.

572 *reminds* LC, etc. (remind 1899, HTC only) This edition follows Ross in
correcting this grammatical slip.

worst excesses of the French Revolution. And I presume
you know what that unfortunate movement led to? As for
the particular locality in which the hand-bag was found, a   575
cloak-room at a railway station might serve to conceal a
social indiscretion—has probably, indeed, been used for
that purpose before now—but it could hardly be regarded
as an assured basis for a recognized position in good
society.   580

JACK

May I ask you then what you would advise me to do? I need
hardly say I would do anything in the world to ensure
Gwendolen's happiness.

LADY BRACKNELL

I would strongly advise you, Mr Worthing, to try and
acquire some relations as soon as possible, and to make a   585
definite effort to produce at any rate one parent of either
sex, before the season is quite over.

JACK

Well, I don't see how I could possibly manage to do that. I
can produce the hand-bag at any moment. It is in my
dressing-room at home. I really think that should satisfy   590
you, Lady Bracknell.

LADY BRACKNELL

Me, sir! What has it to do with me? You can hardly imagine
that I and Lord Bracknell would dream of allowing our
only daughter—a girl brought up with the utmost
care—to marry into a cloak-room, and form an alliance   595
with a parcel? Good morning, Mr Worthing!

LADY BRACKNELL *sweeps out in majestic indignation*

JACK

Good morning! (ALGERNON, *from the other room, strikes up
the Wedding March.* JACK *looks perfectly furious, and goes to
the door*) For goodness' sake don't play that ghastly tune,
Algy! How idiotic you are!

The music stops, and ALGERNON *enters cheerily*

ALGERNON

Didn't it go off all right, old boy? You don't mean to say   600

---

590 *dressing-room* 1899 (bedroom PR, HTC1, etc.) Alexander omits the whole
    sentence.
592–6 See Appendix IV, p. 118.
597 s.d. *Wedding March* Presumably Mendelssohn's, from his incidental music to *A
    Midsummer Night's Dream.*

Gwendolen refused you? I know it is a way she has. She is always refusing people. I think it is most ill-natured of her.

JACK

Oh, Gwendolen is as right as a trivet. As far as she is concerned, we are engaged. Her mother is perfectly unbearable. Never met such a Gorgon—I don't really 605 know what a Gorgon is like, but I am quite sure that Lady Bracknell is one. In any case, she is a monster, without being a myth, which is rather unfair. I beg your pardon, Algy, I suppose I shouldn't talk about your own aunt in that way before you. 610

ALGERNON

My dear boy, I love hearing my relations abused. It is the only thing that makes me put up with them at all. Relations are simply a tedious pack of people, who haven't got the remotest knowledge of how to live, nor the smallest instinct about when to die. 615

JACK

Oh, that is nonsense!

ALGERNON

It isn't!

JACK

Well, I won't argue about the matter. You always want to argue about things.

ALGERNON

That is exactly what things were originally made for. 620

JACK

Upon my word, if I thought that, I'd shoot myself—(*A pause*) You don't think there is any chance of Gwendolen becoming like her mother in about a hundred and fifty years, do you Algy?

ALGERNON

All women become like their mothers. That is their 625 tragedy. No man does. That's his.

601–2 *I know ... of her* 1899 (om. HTC, etc.) Added to WD. Alexander has the men take cigarettes during the sequence following, but they do not light them until ll. 639–45.

603 See Appendix IV, p. 118.

605–21 *I don't really know ... I'd shoot myself* 1899, HTC1, etc. (om. HTC only) The MS draft of this passage is longer, but includes these lines.

612–15 See Appendix IV, p. 119.

625–6 In all texts before 1899 this speech is preceded by the s.d. '(*Drawlingly and sententiously*)'. It was deleted from WD.

JACK

Is that clever?

ALGERNON

It is perfectly phrased! and quite as true as any observation in civilized life should be.

JACK

I am sick to death of cleverness. Everybody is clever nowa-   630
days. You can't go anywhere without meeting clever people. The thing has become an absolute public nuisance. I wish to goodness we had a few fools left.

ALGERNON

We have.

JACK

I should extremely like to meet them. What do they talk   635
about?

ALGERNON

The fools? Oh! about the clever people, of course.

JACK

What fools!

ALGERNON

By the way, did you tell Gwendolen the truth about your being Ernest in town, and Jack in the country?   640

JACK (*In a very patronizing manner*)

My dear fellow, the truth isn't quite the sort of thing one tells to a nice sweet refined girl. What extraordinary ideas you have about the way to behave to a woman!

ALGERNON

The only way to behave to a woman is to make love to her if she is pretty, and to someone else if she is plain.   645

JACK

Oh, that is nonsense.

ALGERNON

What about your brother? What about the profligate Ernest?

628–9 *as any observation in civilized life should be* 1899 (as anything in civilized life should be PR; as anything in modern life should be HTC, etc.)

638 See Appendix IV, pp. 119–20.

643 *a woman* 1899, HTC (women HTC1, etc., with appropriate changes in follow-ing line). Altered in WD.

644 *to make love to her* The older, more general sense of 'court, pay amorous attention'. Cf. Grundy's *The New Woman* (Comedy Theatre, September 1894): 'Do you suppose you are the only man that's ever made love to me? It's a man's business to make love, and it's a woman's business to stop him—when he makes love too hard' (Lord Chamberlain's copy, British Library).

JACK

Oh, before the end of the week I shall have got rid of him.
I'll say he died in Paris of apoplexy. Lots of people die of   650
apoplexy, quite suddenly, don't they?

ALGERNON

Yes, but it's hereditary, my dear fellow. It's a sort of thing
that runs in families. You had much better say a severe
chill.

JACK

You are sure a severe chill isn't hereditary, or anything of   655
that kind?

ALGERNON

Of course it isn't!

JACK

Very well, then. My poor brother Ernest is carried off
suddenly in Paris, by a severe chill. That gets rid of him.

ALGERNON

But I thought you said that—Miss Cardew was a little too   660
much interested in your poor brother Ernest? Won't she
feel his loss a good deal?

JACK

Oh, that is all right. Cecily is not a silly romantic girl, I am
glad to say. She has got a capital appetite, goes long walks,
and pays no attention at all to her lessons.   665

ALGERNON

I would rather like to see Cecily.

JACK

I will take very good care you never do. She is excessively
pretty, and she is only just eighteen.

658–9 In the MS draft the speech anticipates Jack's appearance in Act II:

Very well then. That is settled. Ernest is carried off by a severe chill in Paris.
I'll wear mourning for him of course; that would be only decent. I don't at all
mind wearing mourning. I think that all black, with a good pearl pin, rather
smart [*sic*]. Then I'll go down home and break the news to my household. Of
course, I know they will insist on being awfully sympathetic about it. But I
don't mind that. The thing will be forgotten in a week.

661–2 *Won't she ... deal?* (om. HTC, etc.). Added to WD.

665 *pays no attention at all* 1899 (is not at all interested in PR; pays no attention to
HTC; is much interested in HTC1; is very much interested in LC).

667–8 *She is ... eighteen* Cecily has just reached the marriageable age (at which girls
'came out' in Society). In the MS draft this admission is provoked by Algernon's insisting that she is probably plain: 'She is one of those dull, intellectual
girls one meets all over the place. Girls who have got large minds and large
feet ...'

ALGERNON

Have you told Gwendolen yet that you have an excessively
pretty ward who is only just eighteen?   670

JACK

Oh! one doesn't blurt these things out to people. Cecily
and Gwendolen are perfectly certain to be extremely great
friends. I'll bet you anything you like that half an hour after
they have met, they will be calling each other sister.

ALGERNON

Women only do that when they have called each other a lot   675
of other things first. Now, my dear boy, if we want to get a
good table at Willis's, we really must go and dress. Do you
know it is nearly seven?

JACK (*Irritably*)

Oh! it always is nearly seven.

ALGERNON

Well, I'm hungry.   680

JACK

I never knew you when you weren't—

ALGERNON

What shall we do after dinner? Go to a theatre?

JACK

Oh, no! I loathe listening.

ALGERNON

Well, let us go to the Club?

---

670 *ward* 1899, LC, Arents I (young ward HTC, MS)

673 *I'll bet ... that* 1899, HTC (Probably HTC1, etc.) Altered in WD.

677 *Willis's* Alexander alters his typescript to 'the Savoy'. *dress* Evening dress (for
men, black tail-coat and trousers, white shirt, tie, and waistcoat) was usually
worn at better-class restaurants and in the stalls and dress-circle of theatres, as
well as at private functions. At the moment Jack and Algernon are wearing dark
coat, grey trousers, and waistcoat, as is appropriate for afternoon wear and
paying calls.

677–80 *Do you know ... Well* 1899, HTC1, etc. (om. HTC only)

684 *the Club* The old-established clubs were concentrated in the area around Pall
Mall and St James's: 'The West-End, and "Clubland" in particular, was
formerly peopled by a great number of individuals who were without a regular
profession or occupation ... To many of those who were bachelors a club
served as a home—they lived there, lunched there, dined there, and occasionally died there' (Ralph Nevill and Charles Edward Jerningham, *Piccadilly to
Pall Mall*, 1908, pp. 200–1).

JACK
Oh, no! I hate talking.   685
ALGERNON
Well, we might trot round to the Empire at ten?
JACK
Oh, no! I can't bear looking at things. It is so silly.
ALGERNON
Well, what shall we do?
JACK
Nothing!
ALGERNON
It is awfully hard work doing nothing. However, I don't   690
mind hard work where there is no definite object of any
kind.

Enter LANE

LANE
Miss Fairfax.

Enter GWENDOLEN. LANE *goes out*

ALGERNON
Gwendolen, upon my word!
GWENDOLEN
Algy, kindly turn your back. I have something very par-   695
ticular to say to Mr Worthing.

686 *Empire* The Empire Theatre of Varieties, in Leicester Square, one of the
    best-known music-halls in London, especially notable for its spectacular ballets
    with designs by C. Wilhelm. The Promenade at the back of the stalls was
    notorious as a rendezvous for prostitutes, and was the subject of a campaign by
    Mrs Ormiston Chant. The Promenade was for a while partitioned off, but the
    screen was removed in the course of a demonstration in the autumn of 1894.
    The theatre closed in 1927 and was replaced by the Empire Cinema (rebuilt
    1962).
690–2 *It is ... any kind* 1899, HTC1 (om. HTC; LC substitutes 'But' for 'How-
    ever'; Arents has only 'I don't ... any kind'; MS has 'nothing to be gained, and
    no definite').
695–6 In PR there is another sentence at the end of this speech: 'Also pray oblige
    me by looking out of the window'. This also appears in Arents I, altered in
    manuscript to 'in another direction' (although LC reverts to 'window'). In
    HTC 'Pray oblige me by turning your back' is followed by an s.d., 'ALGERNON
    turns away up C.', and Gwendolen moves down to Jack with an exclamation of
    'Ernest!'

ALGERNON

Really, Gwendolen, I don't think I can allow this at all.

GWENDOLEN

Algy, you always adopt a strictly immoral attitude towards life. You are not quite old enough to do that.

ALGERNON *retires to the fireplace*

JACK

My own darling! 700

GWENDOLEN

Ernest, we may never be married. From the expression on mamma's face I fear we never shall. Few parents nowadays pay any regard to what their children say to them. The old-fashioned respect for the young is fast dying out. Whatever influence I ever had over mamma, I lost at the 705 age of three. But although she may prevent us from becoming man and wife, and I may marry someone else, and marry often, nothing that she can possibly do can alter my eternal devotion to you.

JACK

Dear Gwendolen! 710

GWENDOLEN

The story of your romantic origin, as related to me by mamma, with unpleasing comments, has naturally stirred the deeper fibres of my nature. Your Christian name has an irresistible fascination. The simplicity of your character makes you exquisitely incomprehensible to me. Your town 715 address at the Albany I have. What is your address in the country?

JACK

The Manor House, Woolton, Hertfordshire.

ALGERNON, *who has been carefully listening, smiles to himself, and writes the address on his shirt cuff. Then picks up the Railway Guide*

707–8 *and marry often* Wilde reviewed an anonymous work, *How to be Happy though Married*, in the *Pall Mall Gazette* for 18 November 1885. An anecdote that particularly amused him was that of 'the wicked bachelor who spoke of marriage as "a very harmless amusement" and advised a young friend of his to "marry early and marry often"' (*Reviews*, p. 36).

718 s.d. HTC1 has Algernon write on *an envelope at desk*, but all other versions have him use his shirt-cuff, as the business that closes the act demands. Wilde altered WD (which agreed with HTC1) to give the present reading.

GWENDOLEN

There is a good postal service, I suppose? It may be
necessary to do something desperate. That of course will   720
require serious consideration. I will communicate with
you daily.

JACK

My own one!

GWENDOLEN

How long do you remain in town?

JACK

Till Monday.   725

GWENDOLEN

Good! Algy, you may turn round now.

ALGERNON

Thanks, I've turned round already.

GWENDOLEN

You may also ring the bell.

JACK

You will let me see you to your carriage, my own darling?

GWENDOLEN

Certainly.   730

JACK (*To* LANE, *who now enters*)

I will see Miss Fairfax out.

LANE

Yes, sir.   JACK *and* GWENDOLEN *go off*

LANE *presents several letters on a salver to* ALGERNON. *It is to be
surmised that they are bills, as* ALGERNON, *after looking at the
envelopes, tears them up*

ALGERNON

A glass of sherry, Lane.

LANE

Yes, sir.

ALGERNON

To-morrow, Lane, I'm going Bunburying.   735

LANE

Yes, sir.

719–23 (om. HTC) Wilde struck out the speeches in Arents I, but they reappear in
    LC and HTC1.
729 See Appendix IV, p. 120.
732 *Yes, sir* 1899, HTC1 (Thank you, sir HTC1) Alexander adds an s.d.: '*As* LANE
    enters JACK *and* GWENDOLEN *are kissing R.U. As* JACK *looks up he turns his back
    and stands below door R.U.*' In the Theatre Museum prompt-book (?1909),
    which is based on French's edition, the s.d. is cruder: '*They embrace.* LANE
    appears with the letters on tray and is embarrassed at the scene: so are they'.

ALGERNON

I shall probably not be back till Monday. You can put up
my dress clothes, my smoking jacket, and all the Bunbury
suits—

LANE

Yes, sir.   *Handing sherry*   740

ALGERNON

I hope to-morrow will be a fine day, Lane.

LANE

It never is, sir.

ALGERNON

Lane, you're a perfect pessimist.

LANE

I do my best to give satisfaction, sir.

Enter JACK. LANE *goes off*

JACK

There's a sensible, intellectual girl! the only girl I ever   745
cared for in my life. (ALGERNON *is laughing immoderately*)
What on earth are you so amused at?

ALGERNON

Oh, I'm a little anxious about poor Bunbury, that is all.

JACK

If you don't take care, your friend Bunbury will get you
into a serious scrape some day.   750

ALGERNON

I love scrapes. They are the only things that are never
serious.

JACK

Oh, that's nonsense, Algy. You never talk anything but
nonsense.

ALGERNON

Nobody ever does.   755

JACK *looks indignantly at him, and leaves the room.* ALGERNON
lights a cigarette, reads his shirt-cuff, and smiles

Act-Drop

737 *put up* pack
738 *smoking jacket* A jacket for casual indoor wear, usually made of some light
material, with quasi-military frogging and silk (sometimes quilted) facings on
the cuffs and lapels.
755 s.d. See Appendix IV, pp. 120–1.

Act II

*Scene: Garden at the Manor House. A flight of gray stone steps
leads up to the house. The garden, an old-fashioned one, full of
roses. Time of year, July. Basket chairs, and a table covered with
books, are set under a large yew tree.* MISS PRISM *discovered
seated at the table.* CECILY *is at the back watering flowers.*

MISS PRISM (*Calling*)
　　Cecily, Cecily! Surely such a utilitarian occupation as the
　　watering of flowers is rather Moulton's duty than yours?
　　Especially at a moment when intellectual pleasures await
　　you. Your German grammar is on the table. Pray open it at
　　page fifteen. We will repeat yesterday's lesson.　　　　　　　5
CECILY (*Coming over very slowly*)
　　But I don't like German. It isn't at all a becoming
　　language. I know perfectly well that I look quite plain after
　　my German lesson.
MISS PRISM
　　Child, you know how anxious your guardian is that you
　　should improve yourself in every way. He laid particular　　10
　　stress on your German, as he was leaving for town yester-
　　day. Indeed, he always lays stress on your German when
　　he is leaving for town.

1　　s.d. In HTC and earlier texts there are no stone steps and the garden contains
　　yew hedges, rather than a yew tree. An illustration in the *Illustrated London
　　News* (23 February 1895) shows a tree behind the tea-table.
1–4　*such a ... await you* (it is more Moulton's duty to water the roses than yours
　　HTC, LC) The original draft contains a brief appearance for Moulton: Cecily
　　asks him if he would like to take the German lesson in her place, but he declines
　　('I don't hold with them furrin tongues miss') and disappears behind the hedge.
　　This was deleted by hand from the LC typescript. Three further lines for
　　Moulton (at l. 99) appear in the MS draft only.
4–5　*Your German grammar ... yesterday's lesson* 1899, HTC (Your German lesson
　　has been waiting for you now nearly twenty minutes. Pray open your Schiller at
　　once. HTC1, LC). Altered in revisions to WD.
6–7　*a becoming language* Cf. Lady Bracknell's feelings on its respectability (I,
　　369–70). In November 1896 Wilde wrote to Robert Ross from his cell in
　　Reading Gaol: '... I am going to take up the study of German: indeed this
　　seems to be the proper place for such a study' (*Letters*, p. 413).
12–13　*Indeed ... town* (om. HTC, etc.) Added to WD.

CECILY

Dear Uncle Jack is so very serious! Sometimes he is so
serious that I think he cannot be quite well. 15

MISS PRISM (*Drawing herself up*)

Your guardian enjoys the best of health, and his gravity of
demeanour is especially to be commended in one so comparatively young as he is. I know no one who has a higher
sense of duty and responsibility.

CECILY

I suppose that is why he often looks a little bored when we 20
three are together.

MISS PRISM

Cecily! I am surprised at you. Mr Worthing has many
troubles in his life. Idle merriment and triviality would be
out of place in his conversation. You must remember his
constant anxiety about that unfortunate young man his 25
brother.

CECILY

I wish Uncle Jack would allow that unfortunate young
man, his brother, to come down here sometimes. We
might have a good influence over him, Miss Prism. I am
sure you certainly would. You know German, and geo- 30
logy, and things of that kind influence a man very much.

CECILY *begins to write in her diary*

MISS PRISM (*Shaking her head*)

I do not think that even I could produce any effect on a
character that according to his own brother's admission is
irretrievably weak and vacillating. Indeed I am not sure
that I would desire to reclaim him. I am not in favour of 35
this modern mania for turning bad people into good people
at a moment's notice. As a man sows so let him reap. You
must put away your diary, Cecily. I really don't see why
you should keep a diary at all.

CECILY

I keep a diary in order to enter the wonderful secrets of my 40
life. If I didn't write them down I should probably forget
all about them.

MISS PRISM

Memory, my dear Cecily, is the diary that we all carry
about with us.

25–6, 27–8 *that unfortunate young man, his brother* (him HTC, etc.) Altered in
revisions to WD.

37 *As a man ... reap* Cf. Galatians VI, 7: '... whatsoever a man soweth, that shall
he reap'.

CECILY

 Yes, but it usually chronicles the things that have never   45
happened, and couldn't possibly have happened. I believe
that Memory is responsible for nearly all the three-volume
novels that Mudie sends us.

MISS PRISM

 Do not speak slightingly of the three-volume novel, Cecily.
I wrote one myself in earlier days.   50

CECILY

 Did you really, Miss Prism? How wonderfully clever you
are! I hope it did not end happily? I don't like novels that
end happily. They depress me so much.

MISS PRISM

 The good ended happily, and the bad unhappily. That is
what Fiction means.   55

CECILY

 I suppose so. But it seems very unfair. And was your novel
ever published?

MISS PRISM

 Alas! no. The manuscript unfortunately was abandoned. I
use the word in the sense of lost or mislaid. To your work,
child, these speculations are profitless.   60

CECILY (*Smiling*)

 But I see dear Dr Chasuble coming up through the garden.

MISS PRISM (*Rising and advancing*)

 Dr Chasuble! This is indeed a pleasure.

Enter CANON CHASUBLE

CHASUBLE

 And how are we this morning? Miss Prism, you are, I
trust, well?

CECILY

 Miss Prism has just been complaining of a slight headache.   65
I think it would do her so much good to have a short stroll
with you in the Park, Dr Chasuble.

46–8 See Appendix IV, p. 121.
49 *the three-volume novel* 1899, HTC1, etc. (novels HTC only).
51–6 *Did you really . . . And was* (Was HTC) Miss Prism's definition of fiction was
  added to WD.
58 *Alas! no* (No HTC, etc.) In Alexander's notes Cecily '*Rises, looks astonished*' at
  'abandoned'.
63 In HTC Chasuble shakes hands with Cecily and Miss Prism.

MISS PRISM

Cecily, I have not mentioned anything about a headache.

CECILY

No, dear Miss Prism, I know that, but I felt instinctively
that you had a headache. Indeed I was thinking about that,   70
and not about my German lesson, when the Rector came
in.

CHASUBLE

I hope, Cecily, you are not inattentive.

CECILY

Oh, I am afraid I am.

CHASUBLE

That is strange. Were I fortunate enough to be Miss   75
Prism's pupil, I would hang upon her lips. (MISS PRISM
glares) I spoke metaphorically.—My metaphor was drawn
from bees. Ahem! Mr Worthing, I suppose, has not
returned from town yet?

MISS PRISM

We do not expect him till Monday afternoon.   80

CHASUBLE

Ah yes, he usually likes to spend his Sunday in London.
He is not one of those whose sole aim is enjoyment, as, by
all accounts, that unfortunate young man his brother
seems to be. But I must not disturb Egeria and her pupil
any longer.   85

MISS PRISM

Egeria? My name is Laetitia, Doctor.

CHASUBLE (*Bowing*)

A classical allusion merely, drawn from the Pagan authors.
I shall see you both no doubt at Evensong?

MISS PRISM

I think, dear Doctor, I will have a stroll with you. I find I
have a headache after all, and a walk might do it good.   90

CHASUBLE

With pleasure, Miss Prism, with pleasure. We might go as
far as the schools and back.

---

84   *Egeria* The Nymph who, in Roman legend, taught King Numa Pompilius the
principles later enshrined in the city's laws. Nethercot ('Prunes and Miss
Prism') suggests that her associations with law-giving, the chaste goddess
Diana, and discipline are appropriate for Miss Prism. *Laetitia,* Miss Prism's
first name, means 'joy' or 'happiness' in Latin.

MISS PRISM

That would be delightful. Cecily, you will read your
Political Economy in my absence. The chapter on the Fall
of the Rupee you may omit. It is somewhat too sensational. 95
Even these metallic problems have their melodramatic
side.   *Goes down the garden with* DR CHASUBLE

CECILY (*Picks up books and throws them back on table*)
Horrid Political Economy! Horrid Geography! Horrid,
horrid German!

Enter MERRIMAN *with a card on a salver*

MERRIMAN

Mr Ernest Worthing has just driven over from the station. 100
He has brought his luggage with him.

CECILY (*Takes the card and reads it*)
'Mr Ernest Worthing, B. 4, The Albany, W.' Uncle Jack's
brother! Did you tell him Mr Worthing was in town?

MERRIMAN

Yes, Miss. He seemed very much disappointed. I mentioned that you and Miss Prism were in the garden. He said 105
he was anxious to speak to you privately for a moment.

CECILY

Ask Mr Ernest Worthing to come here. I suppose you had
better talk to the housekeeper about a room for him.

MERRIMAN

Yes, Miss.   MERRIMAN *goes off*

CECILY

I have never met any really wicked person before. I feel 110

94 See Appendix IV, pp. 121–22.

94–5 *the Fall of the Rupee* About 1873 the value of the Indian rupee began to fall;
at one point it reached half its pre-1873 sterling value of 2 shillings. In 1893 the
government of India decided to close the mints in an attempt to check its fall.

95–7 *sensational. Even . . . side* (exciting for a young girl HTC, etc.). Final sentence added to WD. Beerbohm bracketed it in his copy of 1899 and noted:
'This sentence should certainly be omitted. It labours, and spoils, the fun of
what goes before. I wonder if Oscar added it for the printed version? I don't
remember hearing it at the St. James's, and I rather think the speech ended
thus: "It is somewhat too sensational for a young girl" '.

100 Franklin Dyall, who played Merriman, recalled the effect of this announcement on the first night: 'This was received with the loudest and most sustained
laugh that I have ever experienced, culminating in a round of applause; and as I
came off Wilde said to me: "I'm so glad you got that laugh. It shows they have
followed the plot" ' (Hesketh Pearson, *The Life of Oscar Wilde*, 1946, p. 257).

rather frightened. I am so afraid he will look just like
everyone else.

Enter ALGERNON, *very gay and debonair*

He does!

ALGERNON (*Raising his hat*)

You are my little cousin Cecily, I'm sure.

CECILY

You are under some strange mistake. I am not little. In   115
fact, I believe I am more than usually tall for my age
(ALGERNON *is rather taken aback*). But I am your cousin
Cecily. You, I see from your card, are Uncle Jack's
brother, my cousin Ernest, my wicked cousin Ernest.

ALGERNON

Oh! I am not really wicked at all, Cousin Cecily. You   120
mustn't think that I am wicked.

CECILY

If you are not, then you have certainly been deceiving us all
in a very inexcusable manner. I hope you have not been
leading a double life, pretending to be wicked and being
really good all the time. That would be hypocrisy.   125

ALGERNON (*Looks at her in amazement*)

Oh! Of course I have been rather reckless.

CECILY

I am glad to hear it.

ALGERNON

In fact, now you mention the subject, I have been very bad
in my own small way.

CECILY

I don't think you should be so proud of that, though I am   130
sure it must have been very pleasant.

ALGERNON

It is much pleasanter being here with you.

CECILY

I can't understand how you are here at all. Uncle Jack
won't be back till Monday afternoon.

114 *little cousin Cecily* 1899, HTC, LC, OCT (little Miss Cecily HTC 1, MS) This
   passage was carefully revised in WD, where Wilde decided on 'cousin Cecily',
   added the repetition in l. 119 ('my cousin Ernest, my wicked cousin Ernest')
   and inserted 'all the time' in l. 125. In HTC and the WD typescript Algernon
   reacts to 'Uncle Jack's Brother' (ll. 118–19) with the echo 'Brother!': this was
   deleted by Wilde but retained by Alexander.
133–4 Alexander has Algernon bring up a chair. He sits at l. 136 ('. . . on Monday
   morning'), but at the mention of Australia he rises and moves right.

ALGERNON

That is a great disappointment. I am obliged to go up by 135
the first train on Monday morning. I have a business
appointment that I am anxious—to miss.

CECILY

Couldn't you miss it anywhere but in London?

ALGERNON

No: the appointment is in London.

CECILY

Well, I know, of course, how important it is not to keep a 140
business engagement, if one wants to retain any sense of
the beauty of life, but still I think you had better wait till
Uncle Jack arrives. I know he wants to speak to you about
your emigrating.

ALGERNON

About my what? 145

CECILY

Your emigrating. He has gone up to buy your outfit.

ALGERNON

I certainly wouldn't let Jack buy my outfit. He has no taste
in neckties at all.

CECILY

I don't think you will require neckties. Uncle Jack is
sending you to Australia. 150

ALGERNON

Australia! I'd sooner die.

CECILY

Well, he said at dinner on Wednesday night, that you
would have to choose between this world, the next world,
and Australia.

ALGERNON

Oh, well! The accounts I have received of Australia and 155
the next world are not particularly encouraging. This
world is good enough for me, Cousin Cecily.

CECILY

Yes, but are you good enough for it?

ALGERNON

I'm afraid I'm not that. That is why I want you to reform

me. You might make that your mission, if you don't mind,   160
Cousin Cecily.

CECILY

I'm afraid I've no time, this afternoon.

ALGERNON

Well, would you mind my reforming myself this afternoon?

CECILY

It is rather Quixotic of you. But I think you should try.   165

ALGERNON

I will. I feel better already.

CECILY

You are looking a little worse.

ALGERNON

That is because I am hungry.

CECILY

How thoughtless of me. I should have remembered that
when one is going to lead an entirely new life, one requires   170
regular and wholesome meals. Won't you come in?

---

160 In the MS draft and LC Cecily's objection to 'You might make that your
mission' is indignant: 'How dare you suggest that I have a mission'. When Algy
protests that he thought every woman had a mission, nowadays, she retorts
'Every female has! No woman—'. Algy claims that he was good, once: 'Oh,
everyone is good until they learn to talk'. Cecily replies:

> Then the world must be very moral. Very few people know how to talk
> nowadays. There is far more culture than conversation. That is why society is
> so dull.

165 *Quixotic* With the impulsive, impractical, and chivalrous idealism of Cer-
vantes's hero in *Don Quixote* (1605, 1615).

171 After *wholesome meals* the MS draft and LC continue:

> ... Miss Prism and I lunch at 2 off some roast mutton.
>
> ALGERNON
>
> I fear that would be too rich for me.
>
> CECILY
>
> Uncle Jack, whose health has been sadly undermined by the late hours you
> keep in town, has been ordered by his London doctor to have *pâté-de-foie-gras*
> sandwiches and 1874 champagne at 12. I don't know if such invalid's fare
> would suit you.
>
> ALGERNON
>
> You are sure the champagne is '74?
>
> CECILY
>
> Poor Uncle Jack has not been allowed to drink anything else for the last two
> years. Even the cheaper clarets are, he tells us, strictly forbidden to him.

This is the basis of Jack's accusation in III, 227–30.

ALGERNON

Thank you. Might I have a button-hole first? I never have
any appetite unless I have a button-hole first.

CECILY

A Maréchal Niel?

ALGERNON

No, I'd sooner have a pink rose.   175

CECILY

Why?   *Cuts a flower*

ALGERNON

Because you are like a pink rose, Cousin Cecily.

CECILY

I don't think it can be right for you to talk to me like that.
Miss Prism never says such things to me.

ALGERNON

Then Miss Prism is a short-sighted old lady. (CECILY *puts*   180
the rose in his button-hole) You are the prettiest girl I ever
saw.

CECILY

Miss Prism says that all good looks are a snare.

ALGERNON

They are a snare that every sensible man would like to be
caught in.   185

CECILY

Oh! I don't think I would care to catch a sensible man. I
shouldn't know what to talk to him about.

They pass into the house. MISS PRISM *and* DR CHASUBLE *return*

MISS PRISM

You are too much alone, dear Dr Chasuble. You should get
married. A misanthrope I can understand—a woman-
thrope, never!   190

---

173 *a button-hole* Cf. 'Phrases and Philosophies for the Use of the Young', published
in *The Chameleon*, December 1894 (*CW*, pp. 1205–6): 'A really well-made
button-hole is the only link between Art and Nature'.

174 *Maréchal Niel* A yellow noisette rose, first introduced into England in the
1860s.

177 *Cousin Cecily* 1899, HTC, LC (Miss Cecily HTC1; Cecily MS).

186–7 *Oh! I don't think ... talk to him about* Alexander adds a reply to this speech:
'Oh, well, I'll soon tell you, if you'll allow me'.

187 s.d. Alexander has Dr Chasuble and Miss Prism enter arm in arm.

189–90 *womanthrope* This new synonym for 'misogynist' appears in *The Critic as
Artist*. Reviewers do not—or should not—read through all the works they
judge: 'If they did so, they would become confirmed misanthropes, or if I may
borrow a phrase from one of the pretty Newnham graduates, confirmed
womanthropes for the rest of their lives' (*Intentions*, p. 131/*CW*, p. 1022).

CHASUBLE (*With a scholar's shudder*)

Believe me, I do not deserve so neologistic a phrase. The precept as well as the practice of the Primitive Church was distinctly against matrimony.

MISS PRISM (*Sententiously*)

That is obviously the reason why the Primitive Church has not lasted up to the present day. And you do not seem to 195 realize, dear Doctor, that by persistently remaining single, a man converts himself into a permanent public temptation. Men should be more careful; this very celibacy leads weaker vessels astray.

CHASUBLE

But is a man not equally attractive when married? 200

MISS PRISM

No married man is ever attractive except to his wife.

CHASUBLE

And often, I've been told, not even to her.

MISS PRISM

That depends on the intellectual sympathies of the woman. Maturity can always be depended on. Ripeness can be trusted. Young women are green. (DR CHASUBLE 205 *starts*) I spoke horticulturally. My metaphor was drawn from fruits. But where is Cecily?

CHASUBLE

Perhaps she followed us to the schools.

Enter JACK *slowly from the back of the garden. He is dressed in the deepest mourning, with crape hat-band and black gloves*

MISS PRISM

Mr Worthing!

CHASUBLE

Mr Worthing? 210

MISS PRISM

This is indeed a surprise. We did not look for you till Monday afternoon.

208 s.d. Alexander's s.d. make sure that the audience catches sight of Jack before he is seen by Miss Prism (who has moved to the right) or Dr Chasuble (over on the left): '*Enter* JACK *slowly from the back of the garden R. He goes C. He is dressed entirely in black.* DR CHASUBLE *and* MISS PRISM *both turn, come down-stage, then toward C., see* JACK *for the first time*'. Chasuble's exclamation (l. 210) is omitted. The entrance is much simpler in LC and the MS draft.

JACK (*Shakes* MISS PRISM's *hand in a tragic manner*)
I have returned sooner than I expected. Dr Chasuble, I
hope you are well?
CHASUBLE
Dear Mr Worthing, I trust this garb of woe does not   215
betoken some terrible calamity?
JACK
My brother.
MISS PRISM
More shameful debts and extravagance?
CHASUBLE
Still leading his life of pleasure?
JACK (*Shaking his head*)
Dead!   220
CHASUBLE
Your brother Ernest dead?
JACK
Quite dead.
MISS PRISM
What a lesson for him! I trust he will profit by it.
CHASUBLE
Mr Worthing, I offer you my sincere condolence. You
have at least the consolation of knowing that you were   225
always the most generous and forgiving of brothers.
JACK
Poor Ernest! He had many faults, but it is a sad, sad blow.
CHASUBLE
Very sad indeed. Were you with him at the end?
JACK
No. He died abroad; in Paris, in fact. I had a telegram last
night from the manager of the Grand Hotel.   230

---

227 *He had many faults* Alexander has Jack take out *'a large black-bordered handkerchief'* and dry his eyes.

230 *from the manager* 1899, HTC1, etc. (from him from the manager HTC only)
His addition seems to imply that in Alexander's performance Jack represented
Ernest as announcing his own death by telegram, then hastily corrected himself. The *Grand Hotel* in the Boulevard des Capucines was one of the most
luxurious in Paris, and is memorably described by George DuMaurier in part
six of his novel *Trilby* (1895). Wilde stayed at the Grand Hotel in
November–December 1891. 'Grand' was added to the WD typescript, making
the reference specific.

CHASUBLE

Was the cause of death mentioned?

JACK

A severe chill, it seems.

MISS PRISM

As a man sows, so shall he reap.

CHASUBLE (*Raising his hand*)

Charity, dear Miss Prism, charity! None of us are perfect.
I myself am peculiarly susceptible to draughts. Will the   235
interment take place here?

JACK

No. He seemed to have expressed a desire to be buried in
Paris.

CHASUBLE

In Paris! (*Shakes his head*) I fear that hardly points to any
very serious state of mind at the last. You would no doubt   240
wish me to make some slight allusion to this tragic domestic affliction next Sunday. (JACK *presses his hand convul-
sively*) My sermon on the meaning of the manna in the
wilderness can be adapted to almost any occasion, joyful,
or, as in the present case, distressing. (*All sigh*) I have   245
preached it at harvest celebrations, christenings, confirma-
tions, on days of humiliation and festal days. The last time
I delivered it was in the Cathedral, as a charity sermon on
behalf of the Society for the Prevention of Discontent
among the Upper Orders. The Bishop, who was present,   250
was much struck by some of the analogies I drew.

JACK

Ah! that reminds me, you mentioned christenings I think,
Dr Chasuble? I suppose you know how to christen all
right? (DR CHASUBLE *looks astounded*) I mean, of course,
you are continually christening, aren't you?   255

MISS PRISM

It is, I regret to say, one of the Rector's most constant
duties in this parish. I have often spoken to the poorer

---

243 *manna* Sustenance provided by God for the children of Israel during their forty
    years in the wilderness (Exodus, XVI).
249–50 *Discontent ... Upper Orders* (Discontent among the Lower Orders PR;
    Discontent among the Higher Orders HTC; Cruelty to Children HTC1, LC,
    OCT, MS) Changed from 'Cruelty to Children' in WD, and further revised in
    proof.

classes on the subject. But they don't seem to know what thrift is.

CHASUBLE

But is there any particular infant in whom you are 260
interested, Mr Worthing? Your brother was, I believe, unmarried, was he not?

JACK

Oh yes.

MISS PRISM (*Bitterly*)

People who live entirely for pleasure usually are.

JACK

But it is not for any child, dear Doctor. I am very fond of 265
children. No! the fact is, I would like to be christened myself, this afternoon, if you have nothing better to do.

CHASUBLE

But surely, Mr Worthing, you have been christened already?

JACK

I don't remember anything about it. 270

CHASUBLE

But have you any grave doubts on the subject?

JACK

I certainly intend to have. Of course I don't know if the thing would bother you in any way, or if you think I am a little too old now.

CHASUBLE

Not at all. The sprinkling, and, indeed, the immersion of 275
adults is a perfectly canonical practice.

258–9 *But . . . thrift is* Wilde added 'in any sphere of conduct' to the end of the sentence in the WD typescript, then deleted his addition. In the MS draft Miss Prism speaks of 'a certain recklessness of living' among the poor. 'Thrift' reflects the frequent exhortations aimed at persuading the poor to exercise self-restraint (not necessarily with the aid of contraceptive techniques) for reasons of economy—arguments derived from Malthus's *Essay on the Principle of Population*, first published in 1798.

260–1 Alexander has Jack register shock at Chasuble's enquiry.

263 *Oh yes* 1899, HTC1, etc. (Quite unmarried HTC only)

272 *I certainly intend to have* (I have the very gravest doubts PR, HTC, etc.) Alexander marks this sentence and the preceding line for omission, but does not strike them out.

JACK

Immersion!

CHASUBLE

You need have no apprehensions. Sprinkling is all that is
necessary, or indeed I think advisable. Our weather is so
changeable. At what hour would you wish the ceremony　280
performed?

JACK

Oh, I might trot round about five if that would suit you.

CHASUBLE

Perfectly, perfectly! In fact I have two similar ceremonies
to perform at that time. A case of twins that occurred
recently in one of the outlying cottages on your own estate.　285
Poor Jenkins the carter, a most hard-working man.

JACK

Oh! I don't see much fun in being christened along with
other babies. It would be childish. Would half-past five
do?

CHASUBLE

Admirably! Admirably! (*Takes out watch*) And now, dear　290
Mr Worthing, I will not intrude any longer into a house of
sorrow. I would merely beg you not to be too much bowed
down by grief. What seem to us bitter trials are often
blessings in disguise.

MISS PRISM

This seems to me a blessing of an extremely obvious kind.　295

Enter CECILY *from the house*

CECILY

Uncle Jack! Oh, I am pleased to see you back. But what
horrid clothes you have got on! Do go and change them.

MISS PRISM

Cecily!

---

277 Alexander adds the exclamation 'Ugh!!!'

278–81 Alexander adds 'Oh, no' to the beginning of the speech. In the MS draft
　　Chasuble shows more of his concern with liturgy and the climate:

> Oh, no. You need have no apprehensions. That form of ritual, strangely
> enough, is now confirmed to certain religious bodies not in direct communion
> with us. Sprinkling is all that is necessary, or indeed, I think, advisable. Our
> weather is so changeable there is great mortality amongst the Baptists. At
> what hour would you wish the ceremony performed?

290 *And now,* In HTC he '*goes to* JACK *and takes his hand*'.

CHASUBLE

My child! my child!

CECILY *goes towards* JACK; *he kisses her brow in a melancholy manner*

CECILY

What is the matter, Uncle Jack? Do look happy! You look 300
as if you had toothache, and I have got such a surprise for
you. Who do you think is in the dining-room? Your
brother!

JACK

Who?

CECILY

Your brother Ernest. He arrived about half an hour ago. 305

JACK

What nonsense! I haven't got a brother.

CECILY

Oh, don't say that. However badly he may have behaved to
you in the past he is still your brother. You couldn't be so
heartless as to disown him. I'll tell him to come out. And
you will shake hands with him, won't you, Uncle Jack? 310
Runs back into the house

CHASUBLE

These are very joyful tidings.

MISS PRISM

After we had all been resigned to his loss, his sudden return
seems to me peculiarly distressing.

JACK

My brother is in the dining-room? I don't know what it all
means. I think it is perfectly absurd. 315

Enter ALGERNON *and* CECILY *hand in hand. They come slowly up
to* JACK

JACK

Good heavens! *Motions* ALGERNON *away*

---

299 *My child! my child!* (om. HTC) Alexander has Jack take out his handkerchief
again and put it to his eyes. The line was added to WD.

316 *Good heavens!* (Go away! HTC) Alexander's s.d. show that Algernon is on the
right, Cecily slightly further left, Jack centre-stage, and Miss Prism and
Chasuble extreme left.

ALGERNON

Brother John, I have come down from town to tell you that
I am very sorry for all the trouble I have given you, and
that I intend to lead a better life in the future.

> JACK *glares at him and does not take his hand*

CECILY

Uncle Jack, you are not going to refuse your own brother's   320
hand?

JACK

Nothing will induce me to take his hand. I think his
coming down here disgraceful. He knows perfectly well
why.

CECILY

Uncle Jack, do be nice. There is some good in everyone.   325
Ernest has just been telling me about his poor invalid
friend Mr Bunbury whom he goes to visit so often. And
surely there must be much good in one who is kind to an
invalid, and leaves the pleasures of London to sit by a bed
of pain.   330

JACK

Oh! he has been talking about Bunbury has he?

CECILY

Yes, he has told me all about poor Mr Bunbury, and his
terrible state of health.

JACK

Bunbury! Well, I won't have him talk to you about Bunbury or about anything else. It is enough to drive one   335
perfectly frantic.

ALGERNON

Of course I admit that the faults were all on my side. But I
must say that I think that Brother John's coldness to me is
peculiarly painful. I expected a more enthusiastic wel-
come, especially considering it is the first time I have come   340
here.

CECILY

Uncle Jack, if you don't shake hands with Ernest I will
never forgive you.

317–19 In the MS draft Dr Chasuble remarks to Miss Prism 'There is good in that
young man. He seems to me sincerely repentant', and she retorts, 'These
sudden conversions do not please me. They belong to dissent. They savour of
the laxity of the Nonconformist'. After Algernon's speech Alexander adds
another 'Go away!' for Jack and the direction '*Kicks out backwards with R. leg*'.

327–36 *whom ... frantic* (om. HTC)—first appears in this form in WD.

342–3 *I will never forgive you* Alexander adds the s.d. '*Pushes* JACK *over R. to* ALGIE'.
Cecily goes over to join Miss Prism and Chasuble on the left.

JACK

Never forgive me?

CECILY

Never, never, never!   345

JACK

Well, this is the last time I shall ever do it.
Shakes hands with ALGERNON *and glares*

CHASUBLE

It's pleasant, is it not, to see so perfect a reconciliation? I
think we might leave the two brothers together.

MISS PRISM

Cecily, you will come with us.

CECILY

Certainly, Miss Prism. My little task of reconciliation is   350
over.

CHASUBLE

You have done a beautiful action to-day, dear child.

MISS PRISM

We must not be premature in our judgements.

CECILY

I feel very happy.   *They all go off*

JACK

You young scoundrel, Algy, you must get out of this place   355
as soon as possible. I don't allow any Bunburying here.

Enter MERRIMAN

MERRIMAN

I have put Mr Ernest's things in the room next to yours,
sir. I suppose that is all right?

JACK

What?

MERRIMAN

Mr Ernest's luggage, sir. I have unpacked it and put it in   360
the room next to your own.

---

344 *Never forgive me?* (om. HTC, etc.). Added to WD.

345 *Never, never,never*! (Never PR; om. HTC, etc.)

346 (I suppose I must then HTC) In HTC he *'squeezes* ALGIE's *hand violently'*. In
PR *'and glares'* is omitted from the s.d.

350–4 *My ... happy* (om. HTC) Alexander has the s.d. 'ALGIE *runs L. to follow*
CECILY. JACK *catches him by the leg with his stick and drags him back'*.

356 Alexander adds the s.d. 'ALGIE *goes to entrance by which* CECILY *has made her exit.*
Whistles and makes signs off stage'.

357 *I have put Mr Ernest's things* (Mr Ernest's things, I have put them HTC only)

JACK

His luggage?

MERRIMAN

Yes, sir. Three portmanteaus, a dressing-case, two hat-boxes, and a large luncheon-basket.

ALGERNON

I am afraid I can't stay more than a week this time.   365

JACK

Merriman, order the dog-cart at once. Mr Ernest has been suddenly called back to town.

MERRIMAN

Yes, sir.   *Goes back into the house*

ALGERNON

What a fearful liar you are, Jack. I have not been called back to town at all.   370

JACK

Yes, you have.

ALGERNON

I haven't heard anyone call me.

JACK

Your duty as a gentleman calls you back.

ALGERNON

My duty as a gentleman has never interfered with my pleasures in the smallest degree.   375

JACK

I can quite understand that.

ALGERNON

Well, Cecily is a darling.

362–4 *His luggage? ... luncheon-basket* (om. HTC, etc.) A man's *dressing-case*, 'ordinarily made of rosewood, mahogany or cormandel wood', was supposed to include 'scent bottles, jars for pomade and tooth-powders, hair brushes and combs, shaving, nail and tooth brushes, razors and strop, nail scissors, button-hook, tweezer, nail file and penknife'. A *luncheon-basket* was 'a convenient little receptacle in which gentlemen who are going out shooting for the day, or artists who wish to sketch, can carry their luncheon with them' (*Cassell's Domestic Dictionary*, n.d.). See Appendix I for the episode in the MS draft in which Gribsby the solicitor serves a writ of attachment on Algernon/Ernest for debt.

364 *large* (om. PR, HTC)

365 In HTC Algernon '*Looks after* CECILY'.

366 *dog-cart* 'This carriage, now extensively in use where rapidity of transit rather than the conveyance of goods is the main object, derives its name from the fact that it was originally adapted as a lightly-made sporting vehicle with a box for carrying pointers' (*Cassell's Domestic Dictionary*).

369–76 *What ... that* (om. HTC, etc.) Added to WD.

JACK

You are not to talk of Miss Cardew like that. I don't like it.

ALGERNON

Well, I don't like your clothes. You look perfectly ridiculous in them. Why on earth don't you go up and change? It   380
is perfectly childish to be in deep mourning for a man who
is actually staying for a whole week in your house as a
guest. I call it grotesque.

JACK

You are certainly not staying with me for a whole week as a
guest or anything else. You have got to leave—by the   385
four-five train.

ALGERNON

I certainly won't leave you so long as you are in mourning.
It would be most unfriendly. If I were in mourning you
would stay with me, I suppose. I should think it very
unkind if you didn't.   390

JACK

Well, will you go if I change my clothes?

ALGERNON

Yes, if you are not too long. I never saw anybody take so
long to dress, and with such little result.

JACK

Well, at any rate, that is better than being always over-
dressed as you are.   395

ALGERNON

If I am occasionally a little over-dressed, I make up for it
by being always immensely over-educated.

JACK

Your vanity is ridiculous, your conduct an outrage, and
your presence in my garden utterly absurd. However, you
have got to catch the four-five, and I hope you will have a   400
pleasant journey back to town. This Bunburying, as you
call it, has not been a great success for you.

    Goes into the house

382, 384 *a whole week* 1899, HTC (a week PR, HTC1, LC, etc.) Altered by Wilde
    in proof.
391–402 *Well . . . for you* (om. HTC) Only ll. 391–3 appear LC and earlier texts.
396–7 Cf. Lord Henry Wotton's description of Lord Grotrian: 'He atones for being
    occasionally somewhat overdressed, by being always absolutely over-educated.
    He is a very modern type' (*Dorian Gray*, ed. Murray, p. 182/ *CW*, p. 138). The
    epigram also appeared in 'Phrases and Philosophies for the Use of the Young'.

ALGERNON

I think it has been a great success. I'm in love with Cecily, and that is everything.

Enter CECILY *at the back of the garden. She picks up the can and begins to water the flowers*

But I must see her before I go, and make arrangements for   405
another Bunbury. Ah, there she is.

CECILY

Oh, I merely came back to water the roses. I thought you were with Uncle Jack.

ALGERNON

He's gone to order the dog-cart for me.

CECILY

Oh, is he going to take you for a nice drive?   410

ALGERNON

He's going to send me away.

CECILY

Then have we got to part?

ALGERNON

I am afraid so. It's a very painful parting.

CECILY

It is always painful to part from people whom one has known for a very brief space of time. The absence of old   415
friends one can endure with equanimity. But even a momentary separation from anyone to whom one has just been introduced is almost unbearable.

ALGERNON

Thank you.

Enter MERRIMAN

MERRIMAN

The dog-cart is at the door, sir.   420
        ALGERNON *looks appealingly at* CECILY

CECILY

It can wait, Merriman—for—five minutes.

MERRIMAN

Yes, miss.   *Exit* MERRIMAN

403–6 See Appendix IV, p. 122.

407 See Appendix IV, pp. 122–3.

415–18 *The absence . . . unbearable* 1899, HTC1, etc. (om. HTC only) Algernon's 'Thank you' is added in HTC1.

ALGERNON

I hope, Cecily, I shall not offend you if I state quite frankly
and openly that you seem to me to be in every way the
visible personification of absolute perfection.   425

CECILY

I think your frankness does you great credit, Ernest. If you
will allow me I will copy your remarks into my diary.
                    Goes over to table and begins writing in diary

ALGERNON

Do you really keep a diary? I'd give anything to look at it.
May I?

CECILY

Oh no. (*Puts her hand over it*) You see, it is simply a very   430
young girl's record of her own thoughts and impressions,
and consequently meant for publication. When it appears
in volume form I hope you will order a copy. But pray,
Ernest, don't stop. I delight in taking down from dictation.
I have reached 'absolute perfection'. You can go on. I am   435
quite ready for more.

ALGERNON (*Somewhat taken aback*)

Ahem! Ahem!

CECILY

Oh, don't cough, Ernest. When one is dictating one should
speak fluently and not cough. Besides, I don't know how to
spell a cough.   *Writes as* ALGERNON *speaks*   440

ALGERNON (*Speaking very rapidly*)

Cecily, ever since I first looked upon your wonderful and
incomparable beauty, I have dared to love you wildly,
passionately, devotedly, hopelessly.

CECILY

I don't think that you should tell me that you love me
wildly, passionately, devotedly, hopelessly. Hopelessly   445
doesn't seem to make much sense, does it?

ALGERNON

Cecily!

432–3 *When it appears ... copy* 1899, HTC (om. HTC1, etc.) Added to WD.

439–40 *Besides, I don't know how to spell a cough* 1899, HTC, Arents III, MS (om.
    HTC1, LC) In the MS draft Cecily adds 'I know it is done by realistic novelists
    who write in horrid dialect, but I don't think it ever looks quite nice on a page'.
    In a review of G. Manville Fenn's *The Master of Ceremonies* (1886) Wilde had
    rebuked the novelist for trying to convey phonetically 'the impression of a lady
    coughing' (*Pall Mall Gazette*, 16 September 1886: *Reviews*, pp. 82–3). For
    LC's version of the dictation sequence (ll. 439–47 of the present edition) see
    Appendix II.

Enter MERRIMAN

MERRIMAN

The dog-cart is waiting, sir.

ALGERNON

Tell it to come round next week, at the same hour.

MERRIMAN (*Looks at* CECILY, *who makes no sign*)

Yes, sir.   MERRIMAN *retires*   450

CECILY

Uncle Jack would be very much annoyed if he knew you
were staying on till next week, at the same hour.

ALGERNON

Oh, I don't care about Jack. I don't care for anybody in the
whole world but you. I love you, Cecily. You will marry
me, won't you?   455

CECILY

You silly boy! Of course. Why, we have been engaged for
the last three months.

ALGERNON

For the last three months?

CECILY

Yes, it will be exactly three months on Thursday.

ALGERNON

But how did we become engaged?   460

CECILY

Well, ever since dear Uncle Jack first confessed to us that
he had a younger brother who was very wicked and bad,
you of course have formed the chief topic of conversation
between myself and Miss Prism. And of course a man who
is much talked about is always very attractive. One feels   465
there must be something in him after all. I daresay it was
foolish of me, but I fell in love with you, Ernest.

ALGERNON

Darling! And when was the engagement actually settled?

CECILY

On the 14th of February last. Worn out by your entire
ignorance of my existence, I determined to end the matter   470
one way or the other, and after a long struggle with myself I
accepted you under this dear old tree here. The next day I

453 *Oh, I don't care about Jack* Alexander's s.d. shows that Algernon is getting
   bolder: he '*leans across table and takes* CECILY's *hands*'.
469 *February* 1899, Arents III, MS (April PR, WD etc.).
472 *under this dear old tree here* 1899, HTC1 (om. HTC; one evening in the garden
   LC, Arents III, MS) Cf. the opening s.d. of the act.

bought this little ring in your name, and this is the little
bangle with the true lovers' knot I promised you always to
wear.   475

ALGERNON

Did I give you this? It's very pretty, isn't it?

CECILY

Yes, you've wonderfully good taste, Ernest. It's the excuse
I've always given for your leading such a bad life. And this
is the box in which I keep all your dear letters.

*Kneels at table, opens box, and produces letters tied up with blue
ribbon*

ALGERNON

My letters! But my own sweet Cecily, I have never written   480
you any letters.

CECILY

You need hardly remind me of that, Ernest. I remember
only too well that I was forced to write your letters for you.
I wrote always three times a week, and sometimes oftener.

ALGERNON

Oh, do let me read them, Cecily!   485

CECILY

Oh, I couldn't possibly. They would make you far too
conceited. (*Replaces box*) The three you wrote me after I
had broken off the engagement are so beautiful, and so
badly spelled, that even now I can hardly read them without crying a little.   490

ALGERNON

But was our engagement ever broken off?

CECILY

Of course it was. On the 22nd of last March. You can see
the entry if you like. (*Shows diary*) 'To-day I broke off my
engagement with Ernest. I feel it is better to do so. The
weather still continues charming'.   495

ALGERNON

But why on earth did you break it off? What had I done? I
had done nothing at all. Cecily, I am very much hurt
indeed to hear you broke it off. Particularly when the
weather was so charming.

CECILY

It would hardly have been a really serious engagement if it   500
hadn't been broken off at least once. But I forgave you
before the week was out.

487–502 *The three . . . was out* 1899, HTC1, etc. (om. HTC).

ALGERNON (*Crossing to her, and kneeling*)
> What a perfect angel you are, Cecily.

CECILY
> You dear romantic boy. (*He kisses her, she puts her fingers*
> *through his hair*) I hope your hair curls naturally, does it?   505

ALGERNON
> Yes, darling, with a little help from others.

CECILY
> I am so glad.

ALGERNON
> You'll never break off our engagement again, Cecily?

CECILY
> I don't think I could break it off now that I have actually
> met you. Besides, of course, there is the question of your   510
> name.

ALGERNON (*Nervously*)
> Yes, of course.

CECILY
> You must not laugh at me, darling, but it had always been a
> girlish dream of mine to love some one whose name was
> Ernest. (ALGERNON *rises,* CECILY *also*) There is something   515
> in that name that seems to inspire absolute confidence. I
> pity any poor married woman whose husband is not called
> Ernest.

ALGERNON
> But, my dear child, do you mean to say you could not love
> me if I had some other name?   520

CECILY
> But what name?

ALGERNON
> Oh, any name you like—Algernon—for instance—

CECILY
> But I don't like the name of Algernon.

ALGERNON
> Well, my own dear, sweet, loving little darling, I really
> can't see why you should object to the name of Algernon. It   525
> is not at all a bad name. In fact, it is rather an aristocratic

519 *child* 1899, HTC1, etc. (Cecily HTC only)

name. Half of the chaps who get into the Bankruptcy Court
are called Algernon. But seriously, Cecily—(*Moving to
her*)—if my name was Algy, couldn't you love me?
CECILY (*Rising*)
   I might respect you, Ernest, I might admire your charac-   530
   ter, but I fear that I should not be able to give you my
   undivided attention.
ALGERNON
   Ahem! Cecily! (*Picking up hat*) Your Rector here is, I
   suppose, thoroughly experienced in the practice of all the
   rites and ceremonials of the Church?   535
CECILY
   Oh yes. Dr Chasuble is a most learned man. He has never
   written a single book, so you can imagine how much he
   knows.
ALGERNON
   I must see him at once on a most important christening—I
   mean on most important business.   540
CECILY
   Oh!
ALGERNON
   I shan't be away more than half an hour.
CECILY
   Considering that we have been engaged since February the
   14th, and that I only met you today for the first time, I
   think it is rather hard that you should leave me for so long a   545
   period as half an hour. Couldn't you make it twenty
   minutes?
ALGERNON
   I'll be back in no time.
                        Kisses her and rushes down the garden

527–8 *Half of the chaps . . . Algernon* 1899 (Half the chaps . . . Algernon HTC; om.
   HTC1) In the MS draft, Arents III, LC and OCT 'In fact it is rather an
   Aristocratic name' is followed by a speech for Cecily: 'I fear it must be. I have
   often come across it in the newspapers in connection with rather painful cases.
   Cases that judges and magistrates have had to decide unfairly'.
541–7 *Oh! . . . twenty minutes?* 1899, HTC1, LC (om. HTC) The passage replaces
   a longer one in Arents III and the MS draft, where Cecily assumes that
   Algernon is going to make arrangements for their wedding. ('Marriage is a very
   serious thing. One has to order a lot of dresses when one's going to get
   married'.)
543 *February* (April PR only)

CECILY

What an impetuous boy he is! I like his hair so much. I
must enter his proposal in my diary.   550

Enter MERRIMAN

MERRIMAN

A Miss Fairfax has just called to see Mr Worthing. On very
important business Miss Fairfax states.

CECILY

Isn't Mr Worthing in his library?

MERRIMAN

Mr Worthing went over in the direction of the Rectory
some time ago.   555

CECILY

Pray ask the lady to come out here; Mr Worthing is sure to
be back soon. And you can bring tea.

MERRIMAN

Yes, miss.   *Goes out*

CECILY

Miss Fairfax! I suppose one of the many good elderly
women who are associated with Uncle Jack in some of his   560
philanthropic work in London. I don't quite like women
who are interested in philanthropic work. I think it is so
forward of them.

Enter MERRIMAN

MERRIMAN

Miss Fairfax.

Enter GWENDOLEN. *Exit* MERRIMAN

CECILY (*Advancing to meet her*)

Pray let me introduce myself to you. My name is Cecily   565
Cardew.

GWENDOLEN

Cecily Cardew? (*Moving to her and shaking hands*) What a
very sweet name! Something tells me that we are going to
be great friends. I like you already more than I can say. My
first impressions of people are never wrong.   570

CECILY

How nice of you to like me so much after we have known
each other such a comparatively short time. Pray sit down.

549 *boy* (fellow HTC only)

GWENDOLEN (*Still standing up*)

I may call you Cecily, may I not?

CECILY

With pleasure!

GWENDOLEN

And you will always call me Gwendolen, won't you? 575

CECILY

If you wish.

GWENDOLEN

Then that is all quite settled, is it not?

CECILY

I hope so.　　　　　　*A pause. They both sit down together*

GWENDOLEN

Perhaps this might be a favourable opportunity for my
mentioning who I am. My father is Lord Bracknell. You 580
have never heard of papa, I suppose?

CECILY

I don't think so.

GWENDOLEN

Outside the family circle, papa, I am glad to say, is entirely
unknown. I think that is quite as it should be. The home
seems to me to be the proper sphere for the man. And 585
certainly once a man begins to neglect his domestic duties
he becomes painfully effeminate, does he not? And I don't
like that. It makes men so very attractive. Cecily, mamma,
whose views on education are remarkably strict, has
brought me up to be extremely short-sighted; it is part of 590
her system; so do you mind my looking at you through my
glasses?

CECILY

Oh! not at all, Gwendolen. I am very fond of being looked
at.

GWENDOLEN (*After examining* CECILY *carefully through a
lorgnette*)

You are here on a short visit I suppose? 595

CECILY

Oh no! I live here.

GWENDOLEN (*Severely*)

Really? Your mother, no doubt, or some female relative of
advanced years, resides here also?

CECILY

Oh no! I have no mother, nor, in fact, any relations.

585–8 *And certainly . . . attractive* (om. HTC)—added by Wilde to the Arents III
typescript.

GWENDOLEN

Indeed?   600

CECILY

My dear guardian, with the assistance of Miss Prism, has
the arduous task of looking after me.

GWENDOLEN

Your guardian?

CECILY

Yes, I am Mr Worthing's ward.

GWENDOLEN

Oh! It is strange he never mentioned to me that he had a   605
ward. How secretive of him! He grows more interesting
hourly. I am not sure, however, that the news inspires me
with feelings of unmixed delight. (*Rising and going to her*) I
am very fond of you, Cecily; I have liked you ever since I
met you! But I am bound to state that now that I know that   610
you are Mr Worthing's ward, I cannot help expressing a
wish you were—well just a little older than you seem to
be—and not quite so very alluring in appearance. In fact,
if I may speak candidly—

CECILY

Pray do! I think that whenever one has anything un-   615
pleasant to say, one should always be quite candid.

GWENDOLEN

Well, to speak with perfect candour, Cecily, I wish that
you were fully forty-two, and more than usually plain for
your age. Ernest has a strong upright nature. He is the very
soul of truth and honour. Disloyalty would be as impos-   620
sible to him as deception. But even men of the noblest
possible moral character are extremely susceptible to the
influence of the physical charms of others. Modern, no less
than Ancient History, supplies us with many most painful
examples of what I refer to. If it were not so, indeed,   625
History would be quite unreadable.

618 *forty-two* (thirty-five HTC, etc.) Altered in WD.

620–1 *Disloyalty . . . deception* (om. HTC, etc.) Added to WD.

623–6 *Modern . . . unreadable* (om. HTC, LC) The MS draft and the Arents III
typescript differ:

The prominent facts of both English and French history, ancient and modern, seem to me to point entirely to that conclusion—and, high-principled
though Ernest is, and I know no one whose principles are so remarkably high
and varied, I see no reason why he should be an exception to what my
researches have told me is undoubtedly the general rule.

(Wilde struck this out in the Arents typescript.)

CECILY

I beg your pardon, Gwendolen, did you say Ernest?

GWENDOLEN

Yes.

CECILY

Oh, but it is not Mr Ernest Worthing who is my guardian.
It is his brother—his elder brother. 630

GWENDOLEN (*Sitting down again*)

Ernest never mentioned to me that he had a brother.

CECILY

I am sorry to say they have not been on good terms for a
long time.

GWENDOLEN

Ah! that accounts for it. And now that I think of it I have
never heard any man mention his brother. The subject 635
seems distasteful to most men. Cecily, you have lifted a
load from my mind. I was growing almost anxious. It
would have been terrible if any cloud had come across a
friendship like ours, would it not? Of course you are quite,
quite sure that it is not Mr Ernest Worthing who is your 640
guardian?

CECILY

Quite sure. (*A pause*) In fact, I am going to be his.

GWENDOLEN (*Enquiringly*)

I beg your pardon?

CECILY (*Rather shy and confidingly*)

Dearest Gwendolen, there is no reason why I should make
a secret of it to you. Our little county newspaper is sure to 645
chronicle the fact next week. Mr Ernest Worthing and I are
engaged to be married.

GWENDOLEN (*Quite politely, rising*)

My darling Cecily, I think there must be some slight error.
Mr Ernest Worthing is engaged to me. The announcement
will appear in the *Morning Post* on Saturday at the latest. 650

636–9 *Cecily ... not?* 1899, HTC1, etc. (om. HTC only)

650 *Morning Post* For many years this, rather than the more expensive (3*d.* as
against 1*d.*) and austere *Times*, was the chief source of fashionable gossip, and
the proper place to announce engagements and marriages. Cf. *An Ideal Husband*, where Lord Goring insists that he never reads *The Times*: 'I only read *The
Morning Post*. All that one should know about modern life is where the
Duchesses are; anything else is quite demoralizing' (*An Ideal Husband*, p.
198/*CW*, p. 538). In the MS draft's version of her Act I interview with Jack,
Lady Bracknell insists that the *Morning Post* 'is the only document of our time
from which the history of the English people in the XIXth century could be
written with any regard to decency'.

CECILY (*Very politely, rising*)

I am afraid you must be under some misconception. Ernest proposed to me exactly ten minutes ago.   *Shows diary*

GWENDOLEN (*Examines diary through her lorgnette carefully*)

It is certainly very curious, for he asked me to be his wife yesterday afternoon at 5.30. If you would care to verify the incident, pray do so. (*Produces diary of her own*) I never   655 travel without my diary. One should always have something sensational to read in the train. I am so sorry, dear Cecily, if it is any disappointment to you, but I am afraid *I* have the prior claim.

CECILY

It would distress me more than I can tell you, dear   660 Gwendolen, if it caused you any mental or physical anguish, but I feel bound to point out that since Ernest proposed to you he clearly has changed his mind.

GWENDOLEN (*Meditatively*)

If the poor fellow has been entrapped into any foolish promise I shall consider it my duty to rescue him at once,   665 and with a firm hand.

CECILY (*Thoughtfully and sadly*)

Whatever unfortunate entanglement my dear boy may have got into, I will never reproach him with it after we are married.

GWENDOLEN

Do you allude to me, Miss Cardew, as an entanglement?   670 You are presumptuous. On an occasion of this kind it becomes more than a moral duty to speak one's mind. It becomes a pleasure.

CECILY

Do you suggest, Miss Fairfax, that I entrapped Ernest into an engagement? How dare you? This is no time for wearing   675 the shallow mask of manners. When I see a spade I call it a spade.

GWENDOLEN (*Satirically*)

I am glad to say that I have never seen a spade. It is obvious that our social spheres have been widely different.

656–7 *One should... in the train* 1899, HTC1, etc. (om. HTC only: earlier texts read 'a train') In HTC Gwendolen moves down right.
660–79 Alexander's s.d. show that this sequence was planned more or less symmetrically, with Gwendolen moving right of centre on l. 670 and Cecily left of centre on her reply. Both are well down-stage.

Enter MERRIMAN, *followed by the* FOOTMAN. *He carries a salver, table cloth, and plate stand.* CECILY *is about to retort. The presence of the servants exercises a restraining influence, under which both girls chafe*

MERRIMAN
Shall I lay tea here as usual, miss? 680
CECILY (*Sternly, in a calm voice*)
Yes, as usual.

MERRIMAN *begins to clear table and lay cloth. A long pause.*
CECILY *and* GWENDOLEN *glare at each other*

GWENDOLEN
Are there many interesting walks in the vicinity, Miss Cardew?
CECILY
Oh! Yes! a great many. From the top of one of the hills quite close one can see five counties. 685
GWENDOLEN
Five counties! I don't think I should like that. I hate crowds.
CECILY (*Sweetly*)
I suppose that is why you live in town?

GWENDOLEN *bites her lip, and beats her foot nervously with her parasol*

GWENDOLEN (*Looking round*)
Quite a well-kept garden this is, Miss Cardew.
CECILY
So glad you like it, Miss Fairfax. 690

682–8 *Are there ... in town?* (om. HTC, LC) Added to WD. The earlier versions set this act indoors, and provide an appropriate exchange:

GWENDOLEN (*Looking round*)
Charming room this is, of yours, Miss Cardew.
CECILY
I am so glad you like it, Miss Fairfax.
GWENDOLEN
I had no idea there was anything approaching good taste in the more remote country districts. It is quite a surprise to me.
CECILY
Ah! I am afraid you judge of the country from what one sees in the large towns, Miss Fairfax. I know most London houses are extremely vulgar.

GWENDOLEN

I had no idea there were any flowers in the country.

CECILY

Oh, flowers are as common here, Miss Fairfax, as people
are in London.

GWENDOLEN

Personally I cannot understand how anybody manages to
exist in the country, if anybody who is anybody does. The   695
country always bores me to death.

CECILY

Ah! This is what the newspapers call agricultural depression, is it not? I believe the aristocracy are suffering
very much from it just at present. It is almost an epidemic
amongst them, I have been told. May I offer you some tea,   700
Miss Fairfax?

GWENDOLEN (*With elaborate politeness*)

Thank you. (*Aside*) Detestable girl! But I require tea!

CECILY (*Sweetly*)

Sugar?

GWENDOLEN (*Superciliously*)

No, thank you. Sugar is not fashionable any more.

CECILY *looks angrily at her, takes up the tongs, and puts four
lumps of sugar into the cup*

CECILY (*Severely*)

Cake or bread and butter?   705

693 After this line Alexander has Merriman re-enter '*carrying wicker cake stand
containing cut bread and butter, plate of muffins, of tea cake, puts it down behind
garden seat.*' This replaces a longer s.d. in the typescript (HTC1) in which a
footman brings the tea things out to Merriman, making two trips to and from
the house in order to do so. LC, Arents III, and the MS draft all have a simpler
direction, bringing Merriman and a footman on together. French's (?1903) has
the HTC1 s.d. word-for-word—which suggests that it was based on a theatre
copy similar to but not identical with Alexander's.

697–8 *agricultural depression* From the early 1870s British agriculture suffered a
severe depression, the principal causes being the increased importation of
cheap foreign produce (especially cereals from North America) and the succes-
sion of bad seasons. Protectionist legislation had been removed and transport
had improved. The great industrial cities were taking more and more workers
from the land.

GWENDOLEN (*In a bored manner*)

Bread and butter, please. Cake is rarely seen at the best houses nowadays.

CECILY (*Cuts a very large slice of cake, and puts it on the tray*)

Hand that to Miss Fairfax.

MERRIMAN *does so, and goes out with* FOOTMAN. GWENDOLEN *drinks the tea and makes a grimace. Puts down cup at once, reaches out her hand to the bread and butter, looks at it, and finds it is cake. Rises in indignation*

GWENDOLEN

You have filled my tea with lumps of sugar, and though I asked most distinctly for bread and butter, you have given 710 me cake. I am known for the gentleness of my disposition, and the extraordinary sweetness of my nature, but I warn you, Miss Cardew, you may go too far.

CECILY (*Rising*)

To save my poor, innocent, trusting boy from the machinations of any other girl there are no lengths to which I 715 would not go.

GWENDOLEN

From the moment I saw you I distrusted you. I felt that you were false and deceitful. I am never deceived in such matters. My first impressions of people are invariably right. 720

CECILY

It seems to me, Miss Fairfax, that I am trespassing on your valuable time. No doubt you have many other calls of a similar character to make in the neighbourhood.

Enter JACK

GWENDOLEN (*Catching sight of him*)

Ernest! My own Ernest!

JACK

Gwendolen! Darling! *Offers to kiss her* 725

GWENDOLEN (*Drawing back*)

A moment! May I ask if you are engaged to be married to this young lady? *Points to* CECILY

JACK (*Laughing*)

To dear little Cecily! Of course not! What could have put such an idea into your pretty little head?

GWENDOLEN

Thank you. You may!   *Offers her cheek*   730
CECILY (*Very sweetly*)

I knew there must be some misunderstanding, Miss Fairfax. The gentleman whose arm is at present round your waist is my dear guardian, Mr John Worthing.

GWENDOLEN

I beg your pardon?

CECILY

This is Uncle Jack.   735

GWENDOLEN (*Receding*)

Jack! Oh!

Enter ALGERNON

CECILY

Here is Ernest.

ALGERNON (*Goes straight over to* CECILY *without noticing anyone else*)

My own love!   *Offers to kiss her*
CECILY (*Drawing back*)

A moment, Ernest! May I ask you—are you engaged to be married to this young lady?   740

ALGERNON (*Looking round*)

To what young lady? Good heavens! Gwendolen!

CECILY

Yes! to good heavens, Gwendolen, I mean to Gwendolen.

ALGERNON (*Laughing*)

Of course not! What could have put such an idea into your pretty little head?

CECILY

Thank you. (*Presenting her cheek to be kissed*) You may.   745
            ALGERNON *kisses her*

GWENDOLEN

I felt there was some slight error, Miss Cardew. The gentleman who is now embracing you is my cousin, Mr Algernon Moncrieff.

---

733 *Mr John Worthing* Alexander adds the s.d.: 'JACK *crosses to* CECILY, *takes her hand and tries to stop her speaking. She disengages herself. He crosses R. to* GWENDOLEN *and tries to explain*'.

736 s.d.   As Algernon enters, Alexander notes that he '*throws hat on seat*'.

742 *Yes ... Gwendolen* (om. HTC only)

CECILY (*Breaking away from* ALGERNON)
Algernon Moncrieff! Oh!

*The two girls move towards each other and put their arms round
each other's waists as if for protection*

CECILY
Are you called Algernon?   750
ALGERNON
I cannot deny it.
CECILY
Oh!
GWENDOLEN
Is your name really John?
JACK (*Standing rather proudly*)
I could deny it if I liked. I could deny anything if I liked.
But my name certainly is John. It has been John for years.   755
CECILY (*To* GWENDOLEN)
A gross deception has been practised on both of us.
GWENDOLEN
My poor wounded Cecily!
CECILY
My sweet wronged Gwendolen!
GWENDOLEN (*Slowly and seriously*)
You will call me sister, will you not?

They embrace. JACK *and* ALGERNON *groan and walk up and down*

CECILY (*Rather brightly*)   760
There is just one question I would like to be allowed to ask
my guardian.
GWENDOLEN
An admirable idea! Mr Worthing, there is just one ques-

749–85 Alexander's s.d. match the verbal patterning of this sequence with a formal
arrangement on stage. The two women move together to the centre as they put
their arms around one another, and the two men stand a little downstage to the
left (Algernon) and right of them. As the women embrace (l. 759 s.d.), the men
'*groan and walk up L. and R.*' and '*Shake fists at each other when up C.*' Jack moves
to the centre for his admission that he never has had a brother (ll. 767–74).

751 *I cannot deny it* A melodramatic s.d. has been crossed out in LC: '*Flinging
himself in despair on the sofa*'.

tion I would like to be permitted to put to you. Where is
your brother Ernest? We are both engaged to be married to
your brother Ernest, so it is a matter of some importance to   765
us to know where your brother Ernest is at present.

JACK (*Slowly and hesitatingly*)

Gwendolen—Cecily—it is very painful for me to be forced
to speak the truth. It is the first time in my life that I have
ever been reduced to such a painful position, and I am
really quite inexperienced in doing anything of the kind.   770
However I will tell you quite frankly that I have no brother
Ernest. I have no brother at all. I never had a brother in my
life, and I certainly have not the smallest intention of ever
having one in the future.

CECILY (*Surprised*)

No brother at all?   775

JACK (*Cheerily*)

None!

GWENDOLEN (*Severely*)

Had you never a brother of any kind?

JACK (*Pleasantly*)

Never. Not even of any kind.

GWENDOLEN

I am afraid it is quite clear, Cecily, that neither of us is
engaged to be married to anyone.   780

CECILY

It is not a very pleasant position for a young girl suddenly
to find herself in. Is it?

763–6 In the MS draft this request is followed by a duet of enquiries concerning
Ernest:

CECILY

We would naturally like to learn something about Ernest's personal appearance.

GWENDOLEN

Any information regarding Ernest's income would be eagerly welcomed.

CECILY

Would the excitements of a country life be too much for Ernest?

GWENDOLEN

Could Ernest stand the quiet of a London season?

CECILY

Is Ernest physically repulsive? Let us know the worst.

GWENDOLEN

Is Ernest socially possible? Let us face facts.

This passage survived into the Arents III typescript, but was omitted in
subsequent versions.

GWENDOLEN

Let us go into the house. They will hardly venture to come
after us there.

CECILY

No, men are so cowardly, aren't they?   785

They retire into the house with scornful looks

JACK

This ghastly state of things is what you call Bunburying, I
suppose?

ALGERNON

Yes, and a perfectly wonderful Bunbury it is. The most
wonderful Bunbury I have ever had in my life.

JACK

Well, you've no right whatsoever to Bunbury here.   790

ALGERNON

That is absurd. One has a right to Bunbury anywhere one
chooses. Every serious Bunburyist knows that.

JACK

Serious Bunburyist! Good heavens!

ALGERNON

Well, one must be serious about something, if one wants to
have any amusement in life. I happen to be serious about   795
Bunburying. What on earth you are serious about I haven't
got the remotest idea. About everything, I should fancy.
You have such an absolutely trivial nature.

JACK

Well, the only small satisfaction I have in the whole of this
wretched business is that your friend Bunbury is quite   800
exploded. You won't be able to run down to the country
quite so often as you used to do, dear Algy. And a very
good thing too.

785 s.d. Alexander's s.d. has the women '*snort*' as they enter the house '*with a
scornful look*'. Then Jack '*hits* ALGIE *in chest with elbow imitating girls' snort*'. In
the MS draft Wilde suggests more elaborate business, which survived through
the Arents III and LC typescripts:

Exeunt into garden, with scornful looks. CECILY *takes a hat from the table as she
passes. Each stops in front of a glass for a moment, and arranges her hair.* JACK *and*
ALGERNON *look at each other for a short time. Then they turn away from each other.*
JACK, *who looks very angry, walks up and down the room. Kicks footstool aside in a
very irritated way.* ALGERNON *goes over to tea-table and eats some muffins after
lifting up the covers of several dishes.*

In French's edition (?1903) the s.d. is cruder than Alexander's:

Exeunt into house with scornful look, R.; ALGY *kicks* JACK, *and* JACK *returns it
spitefully.*

ALGERNON

Your brother is a little off colour, isn't he, dear Jack? You
won't be able to disappear to London quite so frequently as   805
your wicked custom was. And not a bad thing either.

JACK

As for your conduct towards Miss Cardew, I must say that
your taking in a sweet, simple, innocent girl like that is
quite inexcusable. To say nothing of the fact that she is my
ward.   810

ALGERNON

I can see no possible defence at all for your deceiving a
brilliant, clever, thoroughly experienced young lady like
Miss Fairfax. To say nothing of the fact that she is my
cousin.

JACK

I wanted to be engaged to Gwendolen, that is all. I love   815
her.

ALGERNON

Well, I simply wanted to be engaged to Cecily. I adore her.

JACK

There is certainly no chance of your marrying Miss
Cardew.

ALGERNON

I don't think there is much likelihood, Jack, of you and   820
Miss Fairfax being united.

JACK

Well, that is no business of yours.

ALGERNON

If it was my business, I wouldn't talk about it. (*Begins to eat
muffins*) It is very vulgar to talk about one's business. Only
people like stockbrokers do that, and then merely at dinner 825
parties.

815–16 As Jack says 'I love her', Alexander has him place his hand on his heart.
	Jack imitates this action on 'I adore her'.
822–6 *Well . . . dinner parties* This exchange appears in every text from the MS draft
	to the HTC1 typescript, where Alexander marks it for omission. French's
	(?1903) follows him in this, but 1899 and other subsequent editions include it.
	(PR and HTC have 'were' for 'was' in l. 823.) On minding one's own business,
	cf. *Lady Windermere's Fan*, Act III:

	LORD WINDERMERE
	Well, that is no business of yours, is it, Cecil?
	CECIL GRAHAM
	None! That is why it interests me. My own business always bores me to death.
	I prefer other people's.
						(*Lady Windermere's Fan*, pp. 120–1/*CW*, p. 414).

JACK

How you can sit there, calmly eating muffins when we are in this horrible trouble, I can't make out. You seem to me to be perfectly heartless.

ALGERNON

Well, I can't eat muffins in an agitated manner. The butter 830
would probably get on my cuffs. One should always eat muffins quite calmly. It is the only way to eat them.

JACK

I say it's perfectly heartless your eating muffins at all, under the circumstances.

ALGERNON

When I am in trouble, eating is the only thing that consoles 835
me. Indeed, when I am in really great trouble, as anyone who knows me intimately will tell you, I refuse everything except food and drink. At the present moment I am eating muffins because I am unhappy. Besides, I am particularly fond of muffins. *Rising* 840

JACK (*Rising*)

Well, that is no reason why you should eat them all in that greedy way. *Takes muffins from* ALGERNON

ALGERNON (*Offering tea-cake*)

I wish you would have tea-cake instead. I don't like tea-cake.

JACK

Good heavens! I suppose a man may eat his own muffins in 845
his own garden.

ALGERNON

But you have just said it was perfectly heartless to eat muffins.

JACK

I said it was perfectly heartless of you, under the circumstances. That is a very different thing. 850

ALGERNON

That may be, but the muffins are the same.
He seizes the muffin-dish from JACK

---

827 *you can* LC, Arents III (can you 1899, HTC, MS) Ross (1908) follows 1899: French's (?1903) and the current French's edition print these words as they appear in LC.

JACK

Algy, I wish to goodness you would go.

ALGERNON

You can't possibly ask me to go without having some
dinner. It's absurd. I never go without my dinner. No one
ever does, except vegetarians and people like that. Besides   855
I have just made arrangements with Dr Chasuble to be
christened at a quarter to six under the name of Ernest.

JACK

My dear fellow, the sooner you give up that nonsense the
better. I made arrangements this morning with Dr
Chasuble to be christened myself at 5.30, and I naturally   860
will take the name of Ernest. Gwendolen would wish it.
We can't both be christened Ernest. It's absurd. Besides, I
have a perfect right to be christened if I like. There is no
evidence at all that I ever have been christened by anybody. I should think it extremely probable I never was,   865
and so does Dr Chasuble. It is entirely different in your
case. You have been christened already.

ALGERNON

Yes, but I have not been christened for years.

JACK

Yes, but you have been christened. That is the important
thing.   870

ALGERNON

Quite so. So I know my constitution can stand it. If you are
not quite sure about your ever having been christened, I
must say I think it rather dangerous your venturing on it
now. It might make you very unwell. You can hardly have
forgotten that someone very closely connected with you   875
was very nearly carried off this week in Paris by a severe
chill.

853–4 *You can't ... without having some dinner* 1899, HTC1, etc. (I can't go yet, I
      haven't had my dinner HTC)
854–5 *No one ... like that* 1899, HTC1, etc. (om. HTC) In the MS draft the
      sentence ends: 'and people who have got fads' (deleted in Arents III)
865–6 *I should think ... Dr Chasuble* 1899, HTC1, etc. (om. HTC)

JACK

Yes, but you said yourself that a severe chill was not
hereditary.

ALGERNON

It usen't to be, I know—but I daresay it is now. Science is   880
always making wonderful improvements in things.

JACK (*Picking up the muffin-dish*)

Oh, that is nonsense; you are always talking nonsense.

ALGERNON

Jack, you are at the muffins again! I wish you wouldn't.
There are only two left. (*Takes them*) I told you I was
particularly fond of muffins.   885

JACK

But I hate tea-cake.

ALGERNON

Why on earth then do you allow tea-cake to be served up for
your guests? What ideas you have of hospitality!

JACK

Algernon! I have already told you to go. I don't want you
here. Why don't you go!   890

ALGERNON

I haven't quite finished my tea yet! and there is still one
muffin left.

JACK *groans, and sinks into a chair*. ALGERNON *still continues
eating*

Act-Drop

878–82 *Yes, but . . . nonsense* Marked for omission by Alexander. In HTC1 the first
of these speeches has the form common to LC, Arents III, and the MS draft:
'Yes, but you said yourself that it was not hereditary or anything of the kind'.

882 The MS draft at this point moves to an ending for the scene shorter than any
subsequent versions. This was added to by Wilde in manuscript alterations to
the typescript of Arents III, the whole reproduced in LC and finally abandoned in HTC1. The ending of the act as it appears in LC is printed in
Appendix III.

884 *There are only two left* 1899, HTC1 (om. HTC) 1899, HTC1 (om. HTC)

892 See Appendix IV, pp. 124–5.

Act III

Scene: Morning-room at the Manor House. GWENDOLEN *and*
CECILY *are at the window, looking out into the garden.*

GWENDOLEN
The fact that they did not follow us at once into the house,
as anyone else would have done, seems to me to show that
they have some sense of shame left.

CECILY
They have been eating muffins. That looks like repen-
tance.   5

GWENDOLEN (*After a pause*)
They don't seem to notice us at all. Couldn't you cough?

CECILY
But I haven't got a cough.

GWENDOLEN
They're looking at us. What effrontery!

CECILY
They're approaching. That's very forward of them.

GWENDOLEN
Let us preserve a dignified silence.   10

CECILY
Certainly. It's the only thing to do now.

Enter JACK *followed by* ALGERNON. *They whistle some dreadful*
popular air from a British Opera

GWENDOLEN
This dignified silence seems to produce an unpleasant
effect.

---

1   s.d. *Morning-room* The morning-room was quite distinct from the more formal
     drawing-room, showpiece of the house and special province of its lady. *Eti-*
     quette of Good Society suggests that it should be 'cheerful and sunshiny, and
     wear a cosy, domestic look'. Formal calls were made in the afternoon, and
     visitors would be received in the drawing-room: morning calls were customary
     only between intimate friends, who might be welcomed in the 'general tidy
     déshabille' of the morning-room.
7   Alexander notes '*Both cough.* GWEN *first then* CECILY'.
9   Alexander has the women '*turn in and come down L*'.
11   s.d. In Alexander's s.d. the men '*enter R.C. arm in arm. They whistle out of tune*'.
     LC and HTC provide no clue as to which dreadful popular air from a British
     opera Wilde had in mind. In Arents IV and the MS draft the men are already on
     stage when the curtain rises.

CECILY

A most distasteful one.

GWENDOLEN

But we will not be the first to speak. 15

CECILY

Certainly not.

GWENDOLEN

Mr Worthing, I have something very particular to ask you.
Much depends on your reply.

CECILY

Gwendolen, your common sense is invaluable. Mr
Moncrieff, kindly answer me the following question. Why 20
did you pretend to be my guardian's brother?

ALGERNON

In order that I might have an opportunity of meeting you.

CECILY (*To* GWENDOLEN)

That certainly seems a satisfactory explanation, does it
not?

GWENDOLEN

Yes, dear, if you can believe him. 25

CECILY

I don't. But that does not affect the wonderful beauty of his
answer.

GWENDOLEN

True. In matters of grave importance, style, not sincerity
is the vital thing. Mr Worthing, what explanation can you
offer to me for pretending to have a brother? Was it in 30
order that you might have an opportunity of coming up to
town to see me as often as possible?

---

17 Alexander has the s.d. *'crossing* CECILY *and going to* JACK'.

19 *Gwendolen . . . invaluable* 1899, HTC1, etc. (om. HTC only) Alexander has her
   move to Algernon to ask this question: both men are sitting on a settee at the
   right.

23–4 In HTC both girls *'arm in arm move a little L. to C.'*

25–9 *Yes, dear . . . the vital thing* 1899, HTC, etc. (om. HTC1 only)

JACK

Can you doubt it, Miss Fairfax?

GWENDOLEN

I have the gravest doubts upon the subject. But I intend to
crush them. This is not the moment for German sceptic-   35
ism. (*Moving to* CECILY) Their explanations appear to be
quite satisfactory, especially Mr Worthing's. That seems
to me to have the stamp of truth upon it.

CECILY

I am more than content with what Mr Moncrieff said. His
voice alone inspires one with absolute credulity.   40

GWENDOLEN

Then you think we should forgive them?

CECILY

Yes. I mean no.

GWENDOLEN

True! I had forgotten. There are principles at stake that
one cannot surrender. Which of us should tell them? The
task is not a pleasant one.   45

CECILY

Could we not both speak at the same time?

GWENDOLEN

An excellent idea! I nearly always speak at the same time as
other people. Will you take the time from me?

33   Wilde deleted a long direction in WD: Alexander retains only its first instruc-
      tion (up to 'movement'):

      JACK *and* ALGY *both move together like Siamese twins in every movement until both
      say 'christened this afternoon'. First to front of sofa, then fold hands together, then
      raise eyes to ceiling, then sit on sofa, unfold hands, lean back, tilting up legs with
      both feet off ground, then twitch trousers above knee à la dude, so as not to crease
      them, then both feet on ground, fold hands together, on knee and look perfectly
      unconcerned.*

      No subsequent text has this s.d. except French's (?1903), where it appears in
      full. The British Theatre Museum prompt-book based on that edition cuts all
      but the first sentence.

34–8 Alexander omits all but the fourth sentence of this speech ('Their explana-
      tions appear to be quite satisfactory') and has the girls '*go left by turning in arm in
      arm*'. The HTC1 and WD typescripts omit only the first sentence: LC, Arents
      IV, and the MS draft read 'This is no time for scepticism'. 'German' was added
      by Wilde to the proofs of 1899. The reference is probably to the objective,
      scientific spirit associated with German academic research (particularly into
      the historical background and texts of the Bible and Classical literature) rather
      than to German philosophy.

39–40 *I am ... credulity* (om. HTC only)

CECILY

Certainly.   GWENDOLEN *beats time with uplifted finger*

GWENDOLEN *and* CECILY (*Speaking together*)

Your Christian names are still an insuperable barrier. That   50
is all!

JACK *and* ALGERNON (*Speaking together*)

Our Christian names! Is that all? But we are going to be
christened this afternoon.

GWENDOLEN (*To* JACK)

For my sake you are prepared to do this terrible thing?

JACK

I am!   55

CECILY (*To* ALGERNON)

To please me you are ready to face this fearful ordeal?

ALGERNON

I am!

GWENDOLEN

How absurd to talk of the equality of the sexes! Where
questions of self-sacrifice are concerned, men are infinitely
beyond us.   60

JACK

We are! (*Clasps hands with* ALGERNON)

CECILY

They have moments of physical courage of which we
women know absolutely nothing.

GWENDOLEN (*To* JACK)

Darling!

50–65 In the MS draft this passage is longer, and the effect of a 'duet' even more
accentuated. At one point the women divide a sentence between them:

CECILY
But as it is—
GWENDOLEN
We see no possible hope
CECILY
of reconciliation
GWENDOLEN
of any kind.

This passage was included in the Arents IV typescript, but deleted by Wilde.

52–3 Alexander has Jack beat time with his hat. HTC inserts 'Ugh!' after 'Is that
all?' Wilde deleted this in WD.

55, 57 As they make their declarations, Jack and Algernon rise and approach their
fiancées, so that the couples are downstage, right (Jack and Gwendolen) and
half-way upstage, left centre (Algernon and Cecily).

61   *We are!* This first appears as an addition to WD.

ALGERNON (*To* CECILY)
Darling!   *They fall into each other's arms*   65

Enter MERRIMAN. *When he enters he coughs loudly, seeing the
situation*

MERRIMAN
Ahem! Ahem! Lady Bracknell!
JACK
Good heavens!

Enter LADY BRACKNELL. *The couples separate, in alarm. Exit*
MERRIMAN

LADY BRACKNELL
Gwendolen! What does this mean?
GWENDOLEN
Merely that I am engaged to be married to Mr Worthing,
mamma.   70
LADY BRACKNELL
Come here. Sit down. Sit down immediately. Hesitation of
any kind is a sign of mental decay in the young, of physical
weakness in the old. (*Turns to* JACK) Apprised, sir, of my
daughter's sudden flight by her trusty maid, whose confidence I purchased by means of a small coin, I followed her   75
at once by a luggage train. Her unhappy father is, I am glad
to say, under the impression that she is attending a more
than usually lengthy lecture by the University Extension
Scheme on the Influence of a permanent income on
Thought. I do not propose to undeceive him. Indeed I   80
have never undeceived him on any question. I would
consider it wrong. But of course, you will clearly under-

71–3 *Come here . . . Apprised, sir* This passage underwent a good deal of revision.
The 1899 version is essentially that given by Alexander. (He reverses the order
of Lady Bracknell's second sentence: 'a sign of physical weakness in the old,
and mental decay in the young'.) HTC1 is shorter:

Come here at once (*Points to her to sit on sofa, R.C.*) (*Turns to* JACK) Apprised,
sir . . .

The proofs of 1899 read 'Come here. Sit down at once. Sit down at once' and
follow Alexander's order: 'weakness . . . mental decay'. LC and Arents IV have
a protest from Gwendolen, and the MS draft includes a reference to a girl's
engagement coming to her as a surprise—material used in Act I.
76–82 See Appendix IV, p. 125.

stand that all communication between yourself and my
daughter must cease immediately from this moment. On
this point, as indeed on all points, I am firm.   85

JACK

I am engaged to be married to Gwendolen, Lady
Bracknell!

LADY BRACKNELL

You are nothing of the kind, sir. And now, as regards
Algernon!—Algernon!

ALGERNON

Yes, Aunt Augusta.   90

LADY BRACKNELL

May I ask if it is in this house that your invalid friend Mr
Bunbury resides?

ALGERNON (*Stammering*)

Oh! No! Bunbury doesn't live here. Bunbury is somewhere else at present. In fact, Bunbury is dead.

LADY BRACKNELL

Dead! When did Mr Bunbury die? His death must have   95
been extremely sudden.

ALGERNON (*Airily*)

Oh! I killed Bunbury this afternoon. I mean poor Bunbury
died this afternoon.

LADY BRACKNELL

What did he die of?

ALGERNON

Bunbury? Oh, he was quite exploded.   100

LADY BRACKNELL

Exploded! Was he the victim of a revolutionary outrage? I
was not aware that Mr Bunbury was interested in social
legislation. If so, he is well punished for his morbidity.

ALGERNON

My dear Aunt Augusta, I mean he was found out! The
doctors found out that Bunbury could not live, that is what   105
I mean—so Bunbury died.

LADY BRACKNELL

He seems to have had great confidence in the opinion of his
physicians. I am glad, however, that he made up his mind

---

85 Alexander's notes show that by the end of this speech Lady Bracknell is
    centre-stage, with the couples on her right (Gwendolen and Jack) and left. In
    the MS draft and the Arents IV typescript Algernon and Cecily were hidden
    from her (but not from the audience) by a screen until the equivalent of l. 91.

97–106 See Appendix IV, pp. 125–6.

at the last to some definite course of action, and acted under proper medical advice. And now that we have finally 110 got rid of this Mr Bunbury, may I ask, Mr Worthing, who is that young person whose hand my nephew Algernon is now holding in what seems to me a peculiarly unnecessary manner?

JACK

That lady is Miss Cecily Cardew, my ward. 115

LADY BRACKNELL *bows coldly to* CECILY

ALGERNON

I am engaged to be married to Cecily, Aunt Augusta.

LADY BRACKNELL

I beg your pardon?

CECILY

Mr Moncrieff and I are engaged to be married, Lady Bracknell.

LADY BRACKNELL (*With a shiver, crossing to the sofa and sitting down*)

I do not know whether there is anything peculiarly exciting 120 in the air of this particular part of Hertfordshire, but the number of engagements that go on seems to me considerably above the proper average that statistics have laid down for our guidance. I think some preliminary enquiry on my part would not be out of place. Mr Worthing, is Miss 125 Cardew at all connected with any of the larger railway stations in London? I merely desire information. Until yesterday I had no idea that there were any families or persons whose origin was a Terminus.

JACK *looks perfectly furious, but restrains himself*

JACK (*In a clear, cold voice*)

Miss Cardew is the grand-daughter of the late Mr Thomas 130 Cardew of 149, Belgrave Square, S.W.; Gervase Park, Dorking, Surrey; and the Sporran, Fifeshire, N.B.

110–11 *finally ... Bunbury* (buried Mr Bunbury at last HTC, LC; buried this Mr Bunbury at last Arents IV; comfortably buried Mr Bunbury at last MS) Wilde changed 'buried' to 'got rid of' in proof.

125–9 *Mr Worthing ... Terminus* 1899, HTC1, etc. (Mr Worthing, who is Miss Cardew? HTC only) All earlier texts have the full version of Lady Bracknell's enquiry (reading 'I ask merely for' instead of 'I merely desire', which Wilde substituted in proof).

132 1899 and HTC give the Scottish address as printed here: earlier texts read 'the Glen'. *N.B.* (North Britain) was commonly used for postal addresses north of the border. A conscientious Scot might insist that Fife is a kingdom, not a county, and that '-shire' is incorrect.

LADY BRACKNELL

That sounds not unsatisfactory. Three addresses always
inspire confidence, even in tradesmen. But what proof
have I of their authenticity?   135

JACK

I have carefully preserved the Court Guides of the period.
They are open to your inspection, Lady Bracknell.

LADY BRACKNELL (*Grimly*)

I have known strange errors in that publication.

JACK

Miss Cardew's family solicitors are Messrs. Markby,
Markby and Markby.   140

LADY BRACKNELL

Markby, Markby and Markby? A firm of the very highest
position in their profession. Indeed I am told that one of
the Mr Markbys is occasionally to be seen at dinner parties.
So far I am satisfied.

JACK (*Very irritably*)

How extremely kind of you, Lady Bracknell! I have also in   145
my possession, you will be pleased to hear, certificates of
Miss Cardew's birth, baptism, whooping cough, registration, vaccination, confirmation and the measles; both the
German and the English variety.

LADY BRACKNELL

Ah! A life crowded with incident, I see; though perhaps   150
somewhat too exciting for a young girl. I am not myself in
favour of premature experiences. (*Rises, looks at her watch*)

134–5 *even in tradesmen* 1899, HTC (om. HTC1, etc.) Added to WD.
  But what proof have I of their authenticity? 1899, HTC1, etc. (om. HTC only)
136–43 *I have carefully . . . dinner parties* 1899, HTC1, etc. (om. HTC only) In the
  MS draft Mr Markby is seen 'if not at dinner parties, at any rate at evening
  receptions'—a distinction used in Act I to establish the social status of Liberal
  Unionists. Cf. the treatment of the Solicitor in the 'Gribsby' episode from the
  MS draft (Appendix I) and the snobbish Mrs Vane in *Dorian Gray*, chapter 5:
  'Solicitors are a very respectable class, and in the country often dine with the
  best families' (ed. Murray, p. 63/*CW*, p. 59).
145 *How extremely kind of you* 1899, HTC1, etc. (om. HTC only) In the list
  following, texts before 1899 place 'registration' after 'birth'. The alteration was
  made by Wilde in the proofs of 1899.
152 In the MS draft Lady Bracknell adds:

  In the life of a well-ordered and well-balanced young woman marriage should
  be the first event of any importance, and the last. But the modern girl, as I am
  now only too well aware, has a mania for collecting experiences. A somewhat
  expensive hobby. The experiences of a modern girl fetch little, when they
  come to be valued.

Gwendolen! the time approaches for our departure. We
have not a moment to lose. As a matter of form, Mr
Worthing, I had better ask you if Miss Cardew has any   155
little fortune?

JACK

Oh! about a hundred and thirty thousand pounds in the
Funds. That is all. Good-bye, Lady Bracknell. So pleased
to have seen you.

LADY BRACKNELL (*Sitting down again*)

A moment, Mr Worthing. A hundred and thirty thousand   160
pounds! And in the Funds! Miss Cardew seems to me a
most attractive young lady, now that I look at her. Few
girls of the present day have any really solid qualities, any
of the qualities that last, and improve with time. We live, I
regret to say, in an age of surfaces. (*To* CECILY) Come over   165
here, dear. (CECILY *goes across*) Pretty child! your dress is
sadly simple, and your hair seems almost as Nature might
have left it. But we can soon alter all that. A thoroughly
experienced French maid produces a really marvellous
result in a very brief space of time. I remember recom-   170
mending one to young Lady Lancing, and after three
months her own husband did not know her.

JACK (*Aside*)

And after six months nobody knew her.

LADY BRACKNELL (*Glares at* JACK *for a few moments. Then bends,
with a practised smile, to* CECILY)

Kindly turn round, sweet child. (CECILY *turns completely
round*) No, the side view is what I want. (CECILY *presents*   175
her profile) Yes, quite as I expected. There are distinct
social possibilities in your profile. The two weak points in
our age are its want of principle and its want of profile. The

---

160–1 *A hundred ... Funds* Government stocks (Consolidated Funds—also known
as 'Consols') yielding an unspectacular but dependable income. Cf. Shaw's
Widowers' Houses (1892). Sartorius has been paying 7 per cent interest to Dr
Trench:

> It really matters nothing to me, Dr Trench, how you decide. I can easily raise
> the money elsewhere and pay you off. Then, since you are resolved to run no
> risks, you can invest your ten thousand pounds in Consols and get two
> hundred and fifty pounds a year for it instead of seven hundred.

(*Plays Unpleasant*, 1931, p. 60)

162–5 *Few girls ... an age of surfaces.* 1899, HTC1, etc. (om. HTC only)
175–80 See Appendix IV, p. 126.

chin a little higher, dear. Style largely depends on the way
the chin is worn. They are worn very high, just at present.   180
Algernon!

ALGERNON

Yes, Aunt Augusta!

LADY BRACKNELL

There are distinct social possibilities in Miss Cardew's
profile.

ALGERNON

Cecily is the sweetest, dearest, prettiest girl in the whole   185
world. And I don't care twopence about social possibilities.

LADY BRACKNELL

Never speak disrespectfully of Society, Algernon. Only
people who can't get into it do that. (*To* CECILY) Dear child,
of course you know that Algernon has nothing but his   190
debts to depend upon. But I do not approve of mercenary
marriages. When I married Lord Bracknell I had no fortune of any kind. But I never dreamed for a moment of
allowing that to stand in my way. Well, I suppose I must
give my consent.   195

ALGERNON

Thank you, Aunt Augusta.

LADY BRACKNELL

Cecily, you may kiss me!

CECILY (*Kisses her*)

Thank you, Lady Bracknell.

LADY BRACKNELL

You may also address me as Aunt Augusta for the future.

CECILY

Thank you, Aunt Augusta.   200

LADY BRACKNELL

The marriage, I think, had better take place quite soon.

179–80 *the way the chin is worn* Cf. Wilde on dress reform, in *Woman's World*,
December 1887:

The fashionable English waist, also, is not merely far too small ... but it is
worn far too low down. I use the expression 'worn' advisedly, for a waist
nowadays seems to be regarded as an article of apparel to be put on when and
where one likes.

(*Reviews*, p. 237)

192–3 In the MS draft Lady Brancaster adds that her husband was 'one of the
wealthiest commoners in England' when they married.
199–200 *You may ... Aunt Augusta* 1899, HTC1, etc. (om. HTC only)

ALGERNON

Thank you, Aunt Augusta.

CECILY

Thank you, Aunt Augusta.

LADY BRACKNELL

To speak frankly, I am not in favour of long engagements.
They give people the opportunity of finding out each   205
other's character before marriage, which I think is never
advisable.

JACK

I beg your pardon for interrupting you, Lady Bracknell,
but this engagement is quite out of the question. I am Miss
Cardew's guardian, and she cannot marry without my   210
consent until she comes of age. That consent I absolutely
decline to give.

LADY BRACKNELL

Upon what grounds may I ask? Algernon is an extremely, I
may almost say an ostentatiously, eligible young man. He
has nothing, but he looks everything. What more can one   215
desire?

JACK

It pains me very much to have to speak frankly to you,
Lady Bracknell, about your nephew, but the fact is that I
do not approve at all of his moral character. I suspect him
of being untruthful.   220

ALGERNON *and* CECILY *look at him in indignant amazement*

LADY BRACKNELL

Untruthful! My nephew Algernon? Impossible! He is an
Oxonian.

JACK

I fear there can be no possible doubt about the matter.
This afternoon, during my temporary absence in London
on an important question of romance, he obtained admis-   225
sion to my house by means of the false pretence of being my
brother. Under an assumed name he drank, I've just been
informed by my butler, an entire pint bottle of my

207 The MS draft contains further reflections on Lord Brancaster's habit of
acquiescence ('It is the keynote of his character').

213–16 *Algernon . . . desire?* 1899, HTC1, etc. (om. HTC only) LC and earlier texts
add: 'To my own knowledge he is on the list of nearly all the mothers in
London'.

221–2 *He is an Oxonian* Added by Wilde in proof Alexander added 'He's an
Oxonian' to his typescript. Algernon has been educated at Oxford.

Perrier-Jouet, Brut, '89; a wine I was specially reserving
for myself. Continuing his disgraceful deception, he suc-   230
ceeded in the course of the afternoon in alienating the
affections of my only ward. He subsequently stayed to tea,
and devoured every single muffin. And what makes his
conduct all the more heartless is, that he was perfectly well
aware from the first that I have no brother, that I never had   235
a brother, and that I don't intend to have a brother, not
even of any kind. I distinctly told him so myself yesterday
afternoon.

LADY BRACKNELL

Ahem! Mr Worthing, after careful consideration I have
decided entirely to overlook my nephew's conduct to you.   240

JACK

That is very generous of you, Lady Bracknell. My own
decision, however, is unalterable. I decline to give my
consent.

LADY BRACKNELL (*To* CECILY)

Come here, sweet child. (CECILY *goes over*) How old are
you, dear?   245

CECILY

Well, I am really only eighteen, but I always admit to
twenty when I go to evening parties.

LADY BRACKNELL

You are perfectly right in making some slight alteration.
Indeed, no woman should ever be quite accurate about her
age. It looks so calculating—(*In a meditative manner*)   250
Eighteen, but admitting to twenty at evening parties. Well,
it will not be very long before you are of age and free from

---

229 *Perrier-Jouet, Brut, '89* ('74 champagne HTC, etc.) An unsweetened champagne bottled by Perrier-Jouet in 1889. Cf. *De Profundis*, where Wilde includes
among the extravagances of his life with Douglas 'The suppers at Willis's, the
special *cuvée* of Perrier-Jouet reserved always for us...' (*Letters*, p. 507).

233 *and devoured every single muffin* 1899 (om. HTC only) The proof of 1899 reads
'and consumed every one of the muffins'.

238 See Appendix IV, pp. 126–7.

248–51 *You are perfectly right ... evening parties* 1899, HTC1, etc. (om. HTC only)
Cf. Lord Illingworth in *A Woman of No Importance*: 'One should never trust a
woman who tells one her real age. A woman who would tell one that, would tell
one anything' (p. 36/*CW*, p. 441). Lord Goring, in *An Ideal Husband*, is
described by a stage direction as '*Thirty-four, but always says he is younger*'
(p. 20/*CW*, p. 488).

the restraints of tutelage. So I don't think your guardian's
consent is, after all, a matter of any importance.

JACK

Pray excuse me, Lady Bracknell, for interrupting you   255
again, but it is only fair to tell you that according to the
terms of her grandfather's will Miss Cardew does not come
legally of age till she is thirty-five.

LADY BRACKNELL

That does not seem to me to be a grave objection. Thirty-
five is a very attractive age. London society is full of   260
women of the very highest birth who have, of their own
free choice, remained thirty-five for years. Lady
Dumbleton is an instance in point. To my own knowledge
she has been thirty-five ever since she arrived at the age of
forty, which was many years ago now. I see no reason why   265
our dear Cecily should not be even still more attractive at
the age you mention than she is at present. There will be a
large accumulation of property.

CECILY

Algy, could you wait for me till I was thirty-five?

ALGERNON

Of course I could, Cecily. You know I could.   270

CECILY

Yes, I felt it instinctively, but I couldn't wait all that time.

253 After 'tutelage' the MS draft adds:

And to speak frankly, I am personally strongly in favour of somewhat lengthy
engagements. People have time to get rid of that demonstrative period of
affection which in married people is always out of place, and indeed, I am glad
to say, practically unknown nowadays in good society at any rate. There is no
reason for impatience of any kind. A few more roses in the garden, and in your
pretty cheeks, and you will be twenty-one, Cecily. At that period Mr Worthing will cease to have the right to exercise any tyrannical supervision over you,
and your little fortune.

This was deleted from the Arents IV typescript: references elsewhere to
married couples flirting (I, 246–52) and long engagements (III, 204–7) made
it redundant.

258 Alexander adds an s.d. 'CECILY pinches JACK's arm'.

262–8 Lady Dumbleton ... property 1899, HTC1 (om. HTC only) After 'many
years ago now' LC and earlier texts insert 'And Lady Dumbleton is very much
admired in the evening' and read 'now' for 'at present' in the sentence following.
The MS draft's lines on long engagements and flirting by married couples (see
note to l. 253 above) were transposed to continue this speech in Wilde's
manuscript alterations to Arents IV, but were discarded in LC.

I hate waiting even five minutes for anybody. It always
makes me rather cross. I am not punctual myself, I know,
but I do like punctuality in others, and waiting, even to be
married, is quite out of the question. 275

ALGERNON

Then what is to be done, Cecily?

CECILY

I don't know, Mr Moncrieff.

LADY BRACKNELL

My dear Mr Worthing, as Miss Cardew states positively
that she cannot wait till she is thirty-five—a remark which
I am bound to say seems to me to show a somewhat 280
impatient nature—I would beg of you to reconsider your
decision.

JACK

But my dear Lady Bracknell, the matter is entirely in your
own hands. The moment you consent to my marriage with
Gwendolen, I will most gladly allow your nephew to form 285
an alliance with my ward.

LADY BRACKNELL (*Rising and drawing herself up*)

You must be quite aware that what you propose is out of
the question.

JACK

Then a passionate celibacy is all that any of us can look
forward to. 290

272–5 *I hate ... question* 1899, HTC1, etc. (om. HTC only)

277 *Mr Moncrieff* 1899, HTC (om. HTC1, etc; added in proof) Alexander marks
the opening of this gulf between Algernon and Cecily by the resumed formality
of her using his surname and a move in which '*she crosses* ALGIE *and goes up L.
ALGIE is up L.C. they talk across table*'.

289–90 *a passionate celibacy* 1899, HTC (a passionate and careful celibacy WD,
HTC1) Wilde struck out 'and careful' in proof: he may have felt that it was
ambiguous, or that it made the line too 'melodramatic'.

290 Alexander's s.d. carries the division between the lovers a stage further: 'JACK
and ALGIE *turn arm in arm and go up to French windows. The girls turn their backs
and sob*'. At this point the MS draft has a sequence in which Cecily makes one
more appeal to Jack, rebuking him for being selfish. He replies that she
obviously doesn't know the meaning of the word: 'A selfish person is surely one
who seeks to keep his joys and sorrows to himself. I am not like that. When I am
unhappy, as I am now, I desire everyone else to share in my unhappiness'.
Cecily asks Gwendolen to appeal to Jack, but she tells him that from admiring
him she has now progressed to adoring him: 'It requires merely physical
courage to sacrifice oneself. To sacrifice others moral courage is necessary'.
The passage was modified in Wilde's alterations to Arents IV, and disappeared
altogether by the time LC was prepared.

LADY BRACKNELL

That is not the destiny I propose for Gwendolen.
Algernon, of course, can choose for himself. (*Pulls out her
watch*) Come, dear; (GWENDOLEN *rises*) we have already
missed five, if not six, trains. To miss any more might
expose us to comment on the platform.   295

Enter DR CHASUBLE

CHASUBLE

Everything is quite ready for the christenings.

LADY BRACKNELL

The christenings, sir! Is not that somewhat premature?

CHASUBLE (*Looking rather puzzled, and pointing to* JACK *and*
ALGERNON)

Both these gentlemen have expressed a desire for immedi-
ate baptism.

LADY BRACKNELL

At their age? The idea is grotesque and irreligious!   300
Algernon, I forbid you to be baptized. I will not hear of
such excesses. Lord Bracknell would be highly displeased
if he learned that that was the way in which you wasted
your time and money.

CHASUBLE

Am I to understand then that there are to be no christen- 305
ings at all this afternoon?

JACK

I don't think that, as things are now, it would be of much
practical value to either of us, Dr Chasuble.

CHASUBLE

I am grieved to hear such sentiments from you, Mr
Worthing. They savour of the heretical views of the   310

293–5 *we have already . . . platform* 1899, HTC1, LC (we must be going HTC; om.
   Arents IV, MS)

297 *The christenings* In the MS draft she adds 'The marriages have not taken place
   yet' (deleted in Arents IV).

310–13 *They savour . . . secular* In the MS draft Dr Chasuble refers Jack to the
   Fathers of the Church, and their opinion that baptism is a new birth. LC
   substitutes:

   However, where adults are concerned, compulsory christening, except in the
   case of savage tribes, is distinctly uncanonical, so I shall return to the church
   at once . . .

   HTC omits the passage, and the reference to Anabaptists (a dissenting sect
   who believed that baptism conferred by the established church was ineffective,
   and that a second baptism was necessary) was added to WD. The Anabaptists
   flourished in Europe in the 16th century, but the name was applied by their
   enemies to contemporary Baptists. (Cf. II 278–81 n. and 317–19 n.)

Anabaptists, views that I have completely refuted in four
of my unpublished sermons. However, as your present
mood seems to be one peculiarly secular, I will return to
the church at once. Indeed, I have just been informed by
the pew-opener that for the last hour and a half Miss Prism 315
has been waiting for me in the vestry.

LADY BRACKNELL (*Starting*)

Miss Prism! Did I hear you mention a Miss Prism?

CHASUBLE

Yes, Lady Bracknell. I am on my way to join her.

LADY BRACKNELL

Pray allow me to detain you for a moment. This matter
may prove to be one of vital importance to Lord Bracknell 320
and myself. Is this Miss Prism a female of repellent aspect,
remotely connected with education?

CHASUBLE (*Somewhat indignantly*)

She is the most cultivated of ladies, and the very picture of
respectability.

LADY BRACKNELL

It is obviously the same person. May I ask what position 325
she holds in your household?

CHASUBLE (*Severely*)

I am a celibate, madam.

JACK (*Interposing*)

Miss Prism, Lady Bracknell, has been for the last three
years Miss Cardew's esteemed governess and valued com-
panion. 330

LADY BRACKNELL

In spite of what I hear of her, I must see her at once. Let
her be sent for.

CHASUBLE (*Looking off*)

She approaches; she is nigh.

Enter MISS PRISM *hurriedly*

MISS PRISM

I was told you expected me in the vestry, dear Canon. I
have been waiting for you there for an hour and three 335
quarters.

---

315 *pew-opener* A person employed to open the doors of private pews for their
occupants.
325 *It is obviously the same person* The s.d. in HTC and earlier texts, '*thoughtfully*',
makes it clear that this line must be spoken without sarcasm.
333 *nigh* 1899, HTC (here HTC1, etc.) Altered in revisions to WD.

Catches sight of LADY BRACKNELL *who has fixed her with a stony glare.* MISS PRISM *grows pale and quails. She looks anxiously round as if desirous to escape*

LADY BRACKNELL (*In a severe, judicial voice*)
Prism! (MISS PRISM *bows her head in shame*) Come here, Prism! (MISS PRISM *approaches in a humble manner*) Prism! Where is that baby? (*General consternation. The* CANON *starts back in horror.* ALGERNON *and* JACK *pretend to be anxious to shield* CECILY *and* GWENDOLEN *from hearing the details of a terrible public scandal*) Twenty-eight years ago,   340
Prism, you left Lord Bracknell's house, Number 104, Upper Grosvenor Street, in charge of a perambulator that contained a baby, of the male sex. You never returned. A few weeks later, through the elaborate investigations of the Metropolitan police, the perambulator was discovered at   345
midnight, standing by itself in a remote corner of Bayswater. It contained the manuscript of a three-volume novel of more than usually revolting sentimentality. (MISS PRISM *starts in involuntary indignation*) But the baby was not there! (*Everyone looks at* MISS PRISM) Prism! Where is that   350
baby?   *A pause*
MISS PRISM
Lady Bracknell, I admit with shame that I do not know. I only wish I did. The plain facts of the case are these. On the morning of the day you mention, a day that is for ever branded on my memory, I prepared as usual to take the   355
baby out in its perambulator. I had also with me a somewhat old, but capacious hand-bag in which I had intended to place the manuscript of a work of fiction that I had written during my few unoccupied hours. In a moment of mental abstraction, for which I never can forgive myself, I   360
deposited the manuscript in the bassinette, and placed the baby in the hand-bag.

---

339 s.d. Alexander has the men '*turn the girls round, their backs to* MISS PRISM'.
340 *Twenty-eight* (thirty-four HTC; twenty-five LC, Arents IV, MS)
346–7 *Bayswater* (Hyde Park PR, HTC, etc.) Altered by Wilde in proof. A fashionable district to the north of Kensington Gardens.
361 *bassinette* perambulator.

JACK (*Who has been listening attentively*)

But where did you deposit the hand-bag?

MISS PRISM

Do not ask me, Mr Worthing.

JACK

Miss Prism, this is a matter of no small importance to me. I   365
insist on knowing where you deposited the hand-bag that
contained that infant.

MISS PRISM

I left it in the cloak-room of one of the larger railway
stations in London.

JACK

What railway station?   370

MISS PRISM (*Quite crushed*)

Victoria. The Brighton line.   *Sinks into a chair*

JACK

I must retire to my room for a moment. Gwendolen, wait
here for me.

GWENDOLEN

If you are not too long, I will wait here for you all my life.

Exit JACK *in great excitement*

CHASUBLE

What do you think this means, Lady Bracknell?   375

LADY BRACKNELL

I dare not even suspect, Dr Chasuble. I need hardly tell
you that in families of high position strange coincidences
are not supposed to occur. They are hardly considered the
thing.

*Noises heard overhead as if someone was throwing trunks about.
Everyone looks up*

363 In HTC Jack comes centre to ask this question. In LC and earlier texts Lady
Bracknell interposes:

I do not see how that can matter now. It was, I suppose, left at the offices of
one of those publishers who do not return rejected contributions unless
accompanied by stamps. With your usual carelessness, Prism, I suppose you
never dreamed of putting stamps with the baby. That unfortunate child is
probably at the present moment lying in the waste-paper basket of some large
commercial house.

365 *Miss Prism ... to me* 1899, HTC1, etc. (om. HTC only)

368–71 *I left it ... Brighton line.* 1899, HTC1, LC (In the cloak-room at Victoria
Station. The Brighton line HTC)

372–4 *Gwendolen ... all my life* 1899, HTC1 (om. HTC) Earlier texts differ: 'If you
are not too long' is added in manuscript to Arents IV.

CECILY

Uncle Jack seems strangely agitated.   380

CHASUBLE

Your guardian has a very emotional nature.

LADY BRACKNELL

This noise is extremely unpleasant. It sounds as if he was
having an argument. I dislike arguments of any kind. They
are always vulgar, and often convincing.

CHASUBLE (*Looking up*)

It has stopped now.   *The noise is redoubled* 385

LADY BRACKNELL

I wish he would arrive at some conclusion.

GWENDOLEN

This suspense is terrible. I hope it will last.

Enter JACK *with a hand-bag of black leather in his hand*

JACK (*Rushing over to* MISS PRISM)

Is this the hand-bag, Miss Prism? Examine it carefully
before you speak. The happiness of more than one life
depends on your answer.   390

MISS PRISM (*Calmly*)

It seems to be mine. Yes, here is the injury it received
through the upsetting of a Gower Street omnibus in
younger and happier days. Here is the stain on the lining
caused by the explosion of a temperance beverage, an
incident that occurred at Leamington. And here, on the 395
lock, are my initials. I had forgotten that in an extravagant
mood I had had them placed there. The bag is undoubtedly mine. I am delighted to have it so unexpectedly

---

382–4 *It sounds ... convincing* (om. HTC; It sounds as if he were having an
       argument. I dislike arguments of any kind. They are usually vulgar, and always
       violent HTC1, LC) In the MS draft and Arents IV Lady Brancaster suggests
       that 'it sounds as if he were having an argument with the furniture'. The proof
       reads 'usually vulgar', which Wilde corrected to 'always vulgar'.

387 *This suspense ... last* 1899, HTC1, etc. (om. HTC only).

392 *a Gower Street omnibus* Omnibuses (horse-drawn) were identified by their
     destination, painted on the coachwork, rather than by route-numbers.

393–5 *Here ... Leamington* (om. HTC, LC) Added to WD. Leamington Spa is a
       genteel and thoroughly respectable watering-place in Warwickshire. The
       nature of the temperance beverage is made plain in the MS and Arents IV
       version of this passage: 'Here is the indelible stain left on the lining by the
       accidental explosion of a lemonade bottle, an event that occurred during the
       terribly hot summer of '62'.

restored to me. It has been a great inconvenience being
without it all these years.   400

JACK (*In a pathetic voice*)
Miss Prism, more is restored to you than this hand-bag. I
was the baby you placed in it.

MISS PRISM (*Amazed*)
You?

JACK (*Embracing her*)
Yes—mother!

MISS PRISM (*Recoiling in indignant astonishment*)
Mr Worthing! I am unmarried!   405

JACK
Unmarried! I do not deny that is a serious blow. But after
all, who has the right to cast a stone against one who has
suffered? Cannot repentance wipe out an act of folly? Why
should there be one law for men, and another for women?
Mother, I forgive you.   *Tries to embrace her again* 410

MISS PRISM (*Still more indignant*)
Mr Worthing, there is some error. (*Pointing to* LADY
BRACKNELL) There is the lady who can tell you who you
really are.

JACK (*After a pause*)
Lady Bracknell, I hate to seem inquisitive, but would you
kindly inform me who I am?   415

LADY BRACKNELL
I am afraid that the news I have to give you will not
altogether please you. You are the son of my poor sister,
Mrs Moncrieff, and consequently Algernon's elder
brother.

---

407 *cast a stone* (throw HTC, etc.) The phrase's origin is biblical. Christ is asked for
judgement on the woman taken in adultery and insists 'He that is without sin
among you, let him first cast a stone at her' (John VIII, 7).

409–10 *Why ... women?* 1899, etc. (om. HTC1 only) Alexander restores the
sentence, but substitutes 'the man' and 'the woman' for 'man' and 'woman'. Cf.
Hester's speech on the 'double standard' of morality in *A Woman of No Importance*, Act II (p. 72/*CW*, p. 450): 'Set a mark, if you wish, on each, but don't
punish the one and let the other go free. Don't have one law for men and
another for women'. In the MS draft Miss Prism's indignation at this suggestion is expanded upon: 'I have never had a child in my life. The suggestion,
were it not made before such a large number of people, would be almost
indelicate'. The latter of these sentences survived into LC, where the first was
replaced by 'Maternity has never been an incident in my life'.

JACK

Algy's elder brother! Then I have a brother after all. I 420
knew I had a brother! I always said I had a brother!
Cecily,—how could you have ever doubted that I had a
brother. (*Seizes hold of* ALGERNON) Dr Chasuble, my
unfortunate brother. Miss Prism, my unfortunate brother.
Gwendolen, my unfortunate brother. Algy, you young 425
scoundrel, you will have to treat me with more respect in
the future. You have never behaved to me like a brother in
all your life.

ALGERNON

Well, not till today, old boy, I admit. I did my best,
however, though I was out of practice. *Shakes hands* 430

GWENDOLEN (*To* JACK)

My own! But what own are you? What is your Christian
name, now that you have become someone else?

JACK

Good heavens!—I had quite forgotten that point. Your
decision on the subject of my name is irrevocable, I suppose? 435

GWENDOLEN

I never change, except in my affections.

CECILY

What a noble nature you have, Gwendolen!

JACK

Then the question had better be cleared up at once. Aunt
Augusta, a moment. At the time when Miss Prism left me
in the hand-bag, had I been christened already? 440

LADY BRACKNELL

Every luxury that money could buy, including christening, had been lavished upon you by your fond and doting
parents.

JACK

Then I was christened! That is settled. Now, what name
was I given? Let me know the worst. 445

420–1 *I knew I had a brother!* 1899, HTC1, etc. (om. HTC only)
423–5 *Dr Chasuble ... my unfortunate brother* These three introductions (comically
polite and recalling 'that unfortunate young man, his brother'—Miss Prism's
phrase at II, 25–6) were added to WD, and do not appear in any earlier text. In
the proofs of 1899 the s.d. was omitted.
425–8 *Algy, you young scoundrel ... all your life* 1899, HTC1, etc. (om. HTC only)
429–30 See Appendix IV, pp. 127–8.
437 *What a noble nature you have, Gwendolen!* (om. HTC, etc.) This line was added
to WD.

LADY BRACKNELL

Being the eldest son you were naturally christened after your father.

JACK (*Irritably*)

Yes, but what was my father's Christian name?

LADY BRACKNELL (*Meditatively*)

I cannot at the present moment recall what the General's Christian name was. But I have no doubt he had one. He 450 was eccentric, I admit. But only in later years. And that was the result of the Indian climate, and marriage, and indigestion, and other things of that kind.

JACK

Algy! Can't you recollect what our father's Christian name was? 455

ALGERNON

My dear boy, we were never even on speaking terms. He died before I was a year old.

JACK

His name would appear in the Army Lists of the period, I suppose, Aunt Augusta?

LADY BRACKNELL

The General was essentially a man of peace, except in his 460 domestic life. But I have no doubt his name would appear in any military directory.

JACK

The Army Lists of the last forty years are here. These delightful records should have been my constant study. (*Rushes to bookcase and tears the books out*) M. 465 Generals—Mallam, Maxbohm, Magley, what ghastly names they have—Markby, Migsby, Mobbs, Moncrieff!

450–3 *He was eccentric . . . of that kind* (om. HTC) Wilde added 'and indigestion' in proof. LC and earlier texts differ:

> I cannot at the present moment recall *what* the General's Christian name was. Your poor dear mother always addressed him as 'General'. That I remember perfectly. Indeed I don't think she would have called him by his Christian name. But I have no doubt that he had one. He was *violent* in his manner, but there was nothing eccentric about him in any way. In *fact* he was rather a martinet about the little details of daily life. Too much so, I used to tell my dear sister.

456–7 *My dear boy . . . a year old* (HTC om. 'even' and adds 'I believe' after 'He died') This and the preceding speech were added to the Arents IV typescript.
458–72 See Appendix IV, p. 128.

Lieutenant 1840, Captain, Lieutenant-Colonel, Colonel,
General 1869, Christian names, Ernest John. (*Puts book
very quietly down and speaks quite calmly*) I always told you,   470
Gwendolen, my name was Ernest, didn't I? Well, it is
Ernest after all. I mean it naturally is Ernest.

LADY BRACKNELL

Yes, I remember now that the General was called Ernest. I
knew I had some particular reason for disliking the name.

GWENDOLEN

Ernest! My own Ernest! I felt from the first that you could   475
have no other name!

JACK

Gwendolen, it is a terrible thing for a man to find out
suddenly that all his life he has been speaking nothing but
the truth. Can you forgive me?

GWENDOLEN

I can. For I feel that you are sure to change.   480

JACK

My own one!

CHASUBLE (*To* MISS PRISM)

Laetitia!   *Embraces her*

MISS PRISM (*Enthusiastically*)

Frederick! At last!

ALGERNON

Cecily! (*Embraces her*) At last!

JACK

Gwendolen! (*Embraces her*) At last!   485

LADY BRACKNELL

My nephew, you seem to be displaying signs of triviality.

---

473 Alexander, having deleted the preceding passage, adds an appeal from
Jack—'Aunt Augusta!'—which stimulates her to an effort of memory.

475–6 *I felt from the first that you could have no other name.* In LC and earlier texts the
speech continues: 'Even all man's useless information, wonderful though it is,
is nothing compared to the instinct of a good woman'.

481–8 The final form of the ending is established in WD, where Wilde adds the 'At
lasts' and inserts 'vital' before the concluding mention of the play's title.
Alexander follows suit, but adds an 'At last!' for Chasuble. In LC and earlier
texts l. 485 is followed by a re-entry of Lady Bracknell (who has left at l. 474)
and the final line is 'I have missed the last train! Oh!' Wilde replaced this with a
'tag' in which the punning title was spoken—a traditional and satisfyingly
formal device to close a comedy. In the final tableau Alexander placed Lady
Bracknell stage-centre, Gwendolen and Jack to her right, Algernon and Cecily
to her left, and Miss Prism and Dr Chasuble to her right but further upstage.

JACK
    On the contrary, Aunt Augusta, I've now realized for the
first time in my life the vital Importance of Being Earnest.

Tableau

Curtain

APPENDIX I

The Gribsby Episode from the Manuscript Draft

The following sequence is transcribed from the manuscript
draft of Act Two (New York Public Library), as reproduced
in Sarah Augusta Dickson, *The Importance of Being Earnest
... As Originally Written by Oscar Wilde* (New York, 2
volumes, 1956). The portion reprinted here corresponds to
ff. 49–67 of the manuscript, and begins with lines 360–1 of
Act II in the present edition.

MERRIMAN

Mr Ernest's luggage, sir. I have unpacked it and put it in
the room next to your own.

ALGY

I am afraid I can't stay more than a week, Jack, this time.

CECILY

A week? Will you really be able to stay over Monday?

ALGY

I think I can manage to stop over Monday, now.

CECILY

I am so glad.

MERRIMAN (*To* ERNEST)

I beg your pardon, sir. There is an elderly gentleman
wishes to see you. He has just co[m]e in a cab from the
station.   *Holds card on salver*

ALGY

To see me?

MERRIMAN

Yes, sir.

ALGY (*Reads card*)

Parker and Gribsby, Solicitors. I don't know anything
about them. Who are they?

JACK (*Takes card*)

Parker and Gribsby: I wonder who they can be [?] I expect
Ernest they have come about some business for your friend
Bunbury. Perhaps Bunbury wants to make his will, and
wishes you to be executor. (*To* MERRIMAN) Show Messrs
Parker and Gribsby in at once.

MERRIMAN

There is only one gentleman in the hall, sir.

JACK

Show either Mr Parker or Mr Gribsby in.

MERRIMAN

Yes, sir.   *Exit*

JACK

I hope, Ernest, that I may rely on the statement you made
to me last week when I finally settled all your bills for you.
I hope you have no outstanding accounts of any kind.

ALGY

I haven't any debts at all, dear Jack. Thanks to your
generosity, I don't owe a penny, except for a few neckties I
believe.

JACK

I am sincerely glad to hear it.

[*Enter* MERRIMAN]

MERRIMAN

Mr Gribsby.

Enter GRIBSBY. [*Exit* MERRIMAN]

GRIBSBY (*To* CANON CHASUBLE)

Mr Ernest Worthing?

PRISM [*Indicating* ALGY]

This is Mr Ernest Worthing.

GRIBSBY

Mr Ernest Worthing?

ALGY

Yes.

GRIBSBY

Of B.4, The Albany—?

ALGY

Yes, that is my address—

GRIBSBY

I am very sorry, Mr Worthing, but we have a writ of
attachment for 20 days against you at the suit of the Savoy
Hotel Co. Limited for £762. 14. 2.

ALGY

What perfect nonsense! I never dine at the Savoy at my
own expense. I always dine at Willis's. It is far more
expensive. I don't owe a penny to the Savoy.

GRIBSBY

The writ is marked as having been [served] on you personally at the Albany on May the 27th. Judgement was
given in default against you on the fifth of June—Since
then we have written to you no less than thirteen times,

without receiving any reply. In the interest of our clients we had no option but to obtain an order for committal of your person. But, no doubt, Mr Worthing, you will be able to settle the account, without any further unpleasantness. Seven and six should be added to the bill of costs for the expense of the cab which was hired for your convenience in case of any necessity of removal, but that I am sure is a contingency that is not likely to occur.

ALGY

Removal! What on earth do you mean by removal? I haven't the smallest intention of going away. I am staying here for a week. I am staying with my brother.

Points to JACK

GRIBSBY (*To* JACK)

Pleased to meet you, sir.

ALGY (*To* GRIBSBY)

If you imagine I am going up to town the moment I arrive you are extremely mistaken.

GRIBSBY

I am merely a Solicitor myself. I do not employ personal violence of any kind. The officer of the Court whose function it is to seize the person of the debtor is waiting in the fly outside. He has considerable experience in these matters. In the point of fact he has arrested in the course of his duties nearly all the younger sons of the aristocracy, as well as several eldest sons, besides of course a good many members of the House of Lords. His style and manner are considered extremely good. Indeed, he looks more like a betting man than a court-official. That is why we always employ him. But no doubt you will prefer to pay the bill.

ALGY

Pay it? How on earth am I going to do that? You don't suppose I have got any money? How perfectly silly you are. No gentleman ever has any money.

GRIBSBY

My experience is that it is usually relations who pay.

JACK

Kindly allow me to see this bill, Mr Gribsby—(*Turns over immense folio*)—£762. 14. 2 since last October. I am bound to say I never saw such reckless extravagance in all my life.

Hands it to DR CHASUBLE

PRISM

£762 for eating! How grossly materialistic! There can be little good in any young man who eats so much, and so often.

CHASUBLE

It certainly is a painful proof of the disgraceful luxury of the age. We are far away from Wordsworth's plain living and high thinking.

JACK

Now, Dr Chasuble[,] do you consider that I am in any way called upon to pay this monstrous account for my brother?

CHASUBLE

I am bound to say that I do not think so. It would be encouraging his profligacy.

PRISM

As a man sows, so let him reap. The proposed incarceration might be most salutary. It is to be regretted that it is only for 20 days.

JACK

I am quite of your opinion.

ALGY

My dear fellow, how ridiculous you are! You know perfectly well that the bill is really yours.

JACK

Mine [?]

ALGY

Yes: you know it is.

CHASUBLE

Mr Worthing, if this is a jest, it is out of place.

PRISM

It is gross effrontery. Just what I expected from him.

CECILY

It is ingratitude. I didn't expect that.

JACK

Never mind what he says. This is the way he always goes on. [To ALGY] You mean to say that you are not Ernest Worthing, residing at B.4, The Albany [?] I wonder, as you are at it, that you don't deny being my brother at all. Why don't you?

ALGY

Oh! I am not going to do that, my dear fellow, it would be absurd. Of course, I'm your brother. And that is why you should pay this bill for me. What is the use of having a brother, if he doesn't pay one's bills for one?

JACK

Personally, if you ask me, I don't see *any* use in having a brother. As for paying your bill I have not the smallest intention of doing anything of the kind. Dr Chasuble, the worthy Rector of this parish, and Miss Prism[,] in whose admirable and sound judgement I place great reliance[,] are both of opinion that incarceration would do you a great deal of good. And I think so too.

GRIBSBY (*Pulls out watch*)

I am sorry to disturb this pleasant family meeting, but time presses. We have to be at Holloway not later than four o'clock; otherwise it is difficult to obtain admission. The rules are very strict.

ALGY

Holloway!

GRIBSBY

It is at Holloway that detentions of this character take place always.

ALGY

Well, I really am not going to be imprisoned in the suburbs for having dined in the West End. It is perfectly ridiculous.

GRIBSBY

The bill is for suppers, not for dinners.

ALGY

I really don't care. All I say is that I am not going to be imprisoned in the suburbs.

GRIBSBY

The surroundings I admit are middle class: but the gaol itself is fashionable and well-aired: and there are ample opportunities of taking exercise at certain stated hours of the day. In the case of a medical certificate[,] which is always easy to obtain[,] the hours can be extended.

ALGY

Exercise! Good God! no gentleman ever takes exercise. You don't seem to understand what a gentleman is.

GRIBSBY

I have met so many of them, sir, that I am afraid I don't. There are the most curious varieties of them. The result of cultivation, no doubt. Will you kindly come now, sir, if it will not be inconvenient to you.

ALGY (*Appealingly*)

Jack!

PRISM

Pray be firm, Mr Worthing.

CHASUBLE

This is an occasion on which any weakness would be out of place. It would be a form of self-deception.

JACK

I am quite firm: and I don't know what weakness or deception of any kind is.

CECILY

Uncle Jack! I think you have a little money of mine haven't you? Let me pay this bill. I wouldn't like your own brother to be in prison.

JACK

Oh! you can't pay it, Cecily, that is nonsense.

CECILY

Then you will, won't you? I think you would be sorry if you thought your own brother was shut up. Of course, I am quite disappointed with him.

JACK

You won't speak to him again, Cecily, will you?

CECILY

Certainly not. Unless, of course[,] he speaks to me first[;] it would be very rude not to answer him.

JACK

Well, I'll take care he doesn't speak to you. I'll take care he doesn't speak to any body in this house. The man should be cut. Mr Gribsby—

GRIBSBY

Yes, sir.

JACK

I'll pay this bill for my brother. It is the last bill I shall ever pay for him too. How much is it?

GRIBSBY

£762. 14. 2. May I ask your full name, sir?

JACK

Mr John Worthing, J.P., the Manor House, Woolton. Does that satisfy you?

GRIBSBY

Oh! certainly, sir, certainly. It was a mere formality. (*To* MISS PRISM) Handsome place. Ah! the cab will be 5/9 extra: hired for the convenience of the client.

JACK

All right.

PRISM

I must say that I think such generosity quite foolish. Especially paying the cab.

CHASUBLE (*With a wave of the hand*)

The heart has its wisdom as well as the head, Miss Prism.

JACK

Payable to Gribsby and Parker I suppose?

GRIBSBY

Yes, sir. Kindly don't cross the cheque. Thank you.

JACK

You are Gribsby aren't you? What is Parker like?

GRIBSBY

I am both, sir. Gribsby when I am on unpleasant business, Parker on occasions of a less severe kind.

JACK

The next time I see you I hope you will be Parker.

GRIBSBY

I hope so, sir. (*To* DR CHASUBLE) Good day. (DR CHASUBLE *bows coldly*) Good day. (MISS PRISM *bows coldly*) Hope I shall have the pleasure of meeting you again.   *To* ALGY

ALGY

I sincerely hope not. What ideas you have of the sort of society a gentleman wants to mix in. No gentleman ever wants to know a Solicitor, who wants to imprison one in the suburbs.

GRIBSBY

Quite so, quite so.

ALGY

By the way, Gribsby. Gribsby, you are not to go back to the station in that cab. That is my cab. It was taken for my convenience. You and the gentleman who looks like the betting man have got to walk to the station, and a very good thing too. Solicitors don't walk nearly enough. They bolt. But they don't walk. I don't know any solicitor who takes sufficient exercise. As a rule they sit in stuffy offices all day long neglecting their business.

JACK

You can take the cab, Mr Gribsby.

GRIBSBY

Thank you, sir.   *Exit*

APPENDIX II

The Dictation Episode (Act II) in the Licensing Copy

The following appears in the licensing copy (LC) after Cecily's speech instructing Algernon not to cough (lines 438–40 of the present edition). It is a slightly revised version of a passage in the MS draft and the Arents III typescript.

ALGERNON (*Speaking very rapidly*)
Miss Cardew, ever since half past two this afternoon, when I first looked upon your wonderful and incomparable beauty, I have not merely been your abject slave and servant, but, soaring upon the pinions of a possibly monstrous ambition, I have dared to love you wildly, passionately, devotedly, hopelessly.

CECILY (*Laying down her pen*)
Oh! Please say that all over again. You speak far too fast and too indistinctly. Kindly say it all over again.

ALGERNON
Ever since it was half past two this afternoon, when I first looked upon your wonderful and incomparable beauty—

CECILY
Yes, I have got that all right.

ALGERNON (*Stammering*)
I—I— (CECILY *lays down her pen and looks reproachfully at him*)
(*Desperately*) I have not merely been your abject slave and servant, but, soaring on the pinions of a possibly monstrous ambition, I have dared to love you wildly, passionately, devotedly, hopelessly. *Takes out his watch and looks at it*

CECILY (*After writing for some time looks up*)
I have not taken down 'hopelessly'. It doesn't seem to make much sense, does it?   *A slight pause*

ALGERNON (*Starting back*)
Cecily!

CECILY
Is that the beginning of an entirely new paragraph? or should it be followed by a note of admiration?

ALGERNON (*Rapidly and romantically*)
It is the beginning of an entirely new existence for me, and

it shall be followed by such notes of admiration that my whole life shall be a subtle and sustained symphony of Love, Praise and Adoration combined.

CECILY

Oh, I don't think *that* makes any sense at *all*. The fact is that men should never dictate to women. They never know *how* to do it, and when they *do* do it, they always say something particularly foolish.

ALGERNON

I don't care whether what I say is foolish or not. All that I know is that I love you, Cecily! I love you! I can't live without you, Cecily! You know I love you. Will you marry me? Will you be my wife?

Rushes over to her and puts his hand on hers

Enter MERRIMAN

MERRIMAN

The dog-cart is waiting, sir.

APPENDIX III

The Conclusion of Act Two in the Licensing Copy

This extract begins at line 878 of the present edition.

JACK

Yes, but you said yourself it was not hereditary, or anything of the kind.

ALGERNON

It usen't to be, I know—but I daresay it *is* now. Science is always making wonderful improvements in things.

JACK

May I ask, Algy, what on earth do you propose to do?

ALGERNON

Nothing. That is what I have been trying to do for the last ten minutes, and you have kept on doing everything in your power to distract my attention from my work.

JACK

Well, *I* shall go into the house and see Gwendolen. I feel quite sure she expects me.

ALGERNON

I know from her extremely cold manner that Cecily expects me, so *I* certainly shan't go into the house. When a man does exactly what a woman expects him to do, she doesn't think much of him. One should always do what a woman doesn't expect, just as one should always say what she doesn't understand. The result is invariably perfect sympathy on both sides.

JACK

Oh, that is nonsense. You are always talking nonsense.

ALGERNON

It is much cleverer to talk nonsense than to listen to it, my dear fellow, and a much rarer thing too, in spite of all the public may say.

JACK

I don't listen to you. I can't listen to you.

ALGERNON

Oh, that is merely false modesty. You know perfectly well you could listen to me if you tried. You always underrate yourself, an absurd thing to do nowadays when there are such a lot of conceited people about. Jack, you are eating the muffins again! I wish you wouldn't. There are only two left. (*Removes plate*) I *told* you I was particularly fond of muffins.

JACK

But I hate tea-cake.

ALGERNON

Why on earth do you allow tea-cake to be served up for your guests, then? What ideas you have of hospitality!

JACK (*Irritably*)

Oh! that is not the point. We are not discussing tea-cake (*Crosses*) Algy! you are perfectly maddening. You can never stick to the point in any conversation.

ALGERNON (*Slowly*)

No: it always hurts me.

JACK

Good heavens! What affectation! I *loathe* affectation!

ALGERNON

Well, my dear fellow, if you don't like affectation I really don't see what you *can* like. Besides, it isn't affectation. The point always *does* hurt me and I hate physical pain of any kind.

JACK (*Glares at* ALGERNON; *walks up and down stage. Finally comes up to table*)

Algy! I have already told you to go. I don't want you here. *Why don't* you go?

ALGERNON

I haven't quite finished my tea yet.   *Takes last muffin*

JACK *groans and sinks down into a chair and buries his face in his hands*

Act-Drop

APPENDIX IV

LONGER TEXTUAL NOTES

I, 164   *B.4, The Albany* 1899, HTC (E.4, The Albany HTC1, LC, etc.) The letter designating the set of rooms was altered to that of an unoccupied apartment (cf. Donohue, 'The First Production of *The Import-ance of Being Earnest* ...' in *Nineteenth Century British Theatre*, ed. Richards and Thomson, 1971, pp. 125–43; p. 129). The sets of rooms in this group of 'bachelor chambers' (on the north side of Pic-cadilly, between Sackville Street and Burlington House) surround a courtyard with a covered walkway down the middle, giving a collegiate atmosphere. In Act II of the MS draft Miss Prism observes that the wicked Ernest must be 'as bad as any young man who has chambers in the Albany, or indeed even in the vicinity of Piccadilly, can possibly be. And that is saying a good deal nowadays, when sin, I am told, has reached the suburbs'. Albany (as it is usually referred to) is a few minutes' walk from Half Moon Street.

I, 214–20   *Modern life ... daily papers* 1899, HTC1, LC, Arents I (om. HTC; MS omits final two sentences) The poor quality of English journalism, especially in its treatment of art and literature, was one of Wilde's favourite topics. In *The Critic as Artist* Ernest refers to 'ridiculous journalism monopolizing the seat of judgement when it should be apologizing in the dock' (*Intentions*, p. 113/*CW*, p. 1015). Mrs Cheveley in *An Ideal Husband* threatens Chiltern with exposure: 'Think of the hypocrite with his greasy smile penning his leading article, and arranging the foulness of the public placard' (p. 48/*CW*, p. 496). The journalists took more than ample revenge for these and similar taunts when Wilde found himself in the dock.
Alexander has Algernon rise as he speaks l. 214 and on 'What you really are is a Bunburyist/he '*goes up C., throws match into fireplace then comes down C. to* JACK'.

Jack remains seated. This gives Jack command of the stage for the next four or five speeches.

I, 592–6   Lady Bracknell's exit required a good deal of attention. In the MS draft and Arents I Jack '*starts indignantly*' at the word 'parcel' (which he later complains about to Algernon) and she crushes him with a conventional dismissal: 'You will, of course, sir, understand that for the future there is to be no communication of any kind between you and Miss Fairfax' (this was later transferred to III). In revision 'a parcel' became 'a gentleman who by his own admission is a form of unclaimed luggage', but LC incorporated the unrevised Arents I version. In WD this was finally discarded, but doubts still lingered, and Alexander changed 'parcel' to 'hand-bag'. He adds an s.d. after 'Me, sir!' for Lady Bracknell to go up-stage to the door, which Jack opens for her: this enables her to make a quick exit. Alexander then cuts Jack's 'Good morning!' and has him close the door and come down to the table to pick up his gloves—probably to allow for a round of applause after Lady Bracknell leaves the stage.

I, 603   *right as a trivet* A trivet was originally a three-legged stand, and the proverbial phrase alludes to its always standing firmly on its three legs. The conversation is considerably different in the MS draft. Jack says that he is sure Algernon is going to tell him he will make Gwendolen a good husband:

ALGERNON

Oh, no good chap makes a good husband. If a chap makes a good husband there must have been something rather peculiar about him when he was a bachelor. To be a good husband requires considerable practice.

JACK

I think your views quite idiotic, absurd, and ridiculous. You'll find that out for yourself, too, some day, if you can get a charming good nice sweet girl to accept you. But I don't suppose you ever will be able to do that. I don't suppose you would take the trouble. No, all I said was that no-one likes to be told, formally told, in a serious voice, that it is confidently expected that he will make a good husband. It sounds so tedious and second-rate.

I, 612–15   *Relations ... when to die* In the MS draft Algernon adds a few particulars of his family (Mary Farquhar, Gladys, and Lord Bracknell—'uncle Geoffrey'—who 'isn't half a bad sort in his silly way, considering what a thoroughly typical woman Aunt Augusta is'). He also offers another definition of Relations: 'Relations never lend one money, and won't give one credit, even for genius. They are a sort of aggravated form of the public'. Later Jack tells of his interrogation at Lady Bracknell's hands:

> Oh, she was positively violent. I never heard such language in the whole course of my life from anyone. She might just as well have been in a pulpit. I shouldn't be at all surprised if she took to philanthropy or something of the kind and abused her fellow creatures for the rest of her life.

(Cf. Introduction, pp. xxxiii–v) Jack quotes Lady Bracknell's words (especially 'parcel') indignantly, and remarks that whether one has had a father or mother is of little importance: 'Mothers, of course, are all right. They pay a chap's bills and don't bother him. But fathers bother a chap and never pay his bills. I don't know a single chap at the club who speaks to his father ... I bet you anything you like that there is not a single chap, of all the chaps that you and I know, who would be seen walking down St James's Street with his own father'. The worsening relations between Douglas and his father, who had cut off his allowance, are the obvious inspiration for this passage.

I, 638   *What fools!* In the MS draft Jack throws his cigarette away at this line:

JACK
> I am tired of gold-tipped cigarettes. You can get them quite cheap now. No particular advantage in smoking them any longer.

ALGERNON
> Ah! those cigarettes are rather smart. They have got my monogram on each of them.

JACK (*Sneeringly*)
> I don't quite see how that can make the tobacco any better.

ALGERNON
> It does, to me.

JACK

Oh! you are an egotist, Algy.

ALGERNON (*Imperturbable*)

I am, dear boy, that is why my temper is so astoundingly good.

The passage only appears in the MS. Alexander adds business for the lighting of cigarettes in the sequence following l. 639. Algernon lights a match, Jack takes it from him at l. 641, lights his cigarette as he finishes his speech. Algernon makes his next remark, takes the match from Jack, lights his cigarette, and puts the match in the ash-tray on the tea-table.

I, 729   *my own darling* (Miss Fairfax PR, HTC) LC, like earlier texts, has a shorter ending to the act (from l. 725):

GWENDOLEN

Algy, you may turn round now.   *Exit*

JACK

What a splendid creature. Only girl I have ever loved in my life. Let us go off and dine. I'll give you the best dinner in London. What on earth are you laughing at?

ALGERNON

I hope to goodness tomorrow will be a fine day.

JACK

It never is—but what are you going to do tomorrow?

ALGERNON

Tomorrow, my dear boy, I am going Bunburying.

JACK

What nonsense.

ALGERNON

I love nonsense.

Act Drop

I, 755, s.d. The concluding s.d. was added by Wilde to the proof (PR). In HTC1 and WD there is none, but 'Besides, I love nonsense!' is added to the final line: Wilde crossed the words out in revising WD. The earlier typescripts (LC, Arents I) and the MS draft all end with 'I love nonsense'. Alexander added another line and direction: 'The Manor House, Woolton, Hertfordshire. *Drinking as curtain falls*'. In his copy of the 1899 edition (presented and inscribed by Wilde) Max Beerbohm added the words 'And besides, I *love* nonsense!' Below this he wrote:

I have a good verbal and visual memory; and I can still see him raising his glass of sherry as he said them and the curtain fell. I don't see why Oscar cut them for the printed version; for they are just right.

Alexander's alteration of the s.d. at l. 718, where Algernon writes on his cuff, suggests that he read the address from it.

II, 47–8   *three-volume novels that Mudie sends us* (most interesting recent novels HTC; three-volume novels the circulating library sends down to us HTC1; three-volume novels which the circulating library sends us LC) Subscribers to Mudie's circulating library could arrange to be sent a monthly box of the latest publications. On the three-volume novel (a form associated with this mode of distribution, and somewhat outmoded by the mid-1890s), cf. Gilbert's remarks in *The Critic as Artist*: 'Anybody can write a three-volume novel. It merely requires a complete ignorance of both life and literature' (*Intentions*, p. 130/*CW*, p. 1022). In the MS draft Cecily expresses her belief that Memory is responsible for 'nearly all the three-volume novels that every cultivated woman writes now-a-days, and that no cultivated man ever reads'; Miss Prism says that her effort in this *genre* was connected with 'the one great tragedy' of her life; Cecily adds:

How very strange! I knew that three-volume novels often saddened the lives of other people. But I had no idea that to write one was a tragedy. Though now that I think of it I feel it must be true.

II, 94   *Political Economy* An unusual element in the curriculum of a governess and her pupil. In the MS draft Chasuble comments on this and adds:

... I suppose you know all about the relations between Capital and Labour. I wish I did. I am compelled, like most of my brother clergy, to treat scientific subjects from the point of view of sentiment. But that is more impressive I think. Accurate knowledge is out of place in a pulpit. It is secular.

CECILY

I am afraid I'm not learned at all. All I know is about the relations between Capital and Idleness—and that is merely from observation, so I don't suppose it is true.

MISS PRISM

Cecily, that sounds like Socialism. And I suppose you know where Socialism leads to?

CECILY

Oh yes, that leads to Rational Dress, Miss Prism. And I suppose that when a woman is dressed rationally, she is treated rationally—She certainly deserves to be.

(The movement for Rational Dress—fashions for women that allowed greater freedom of movement and were more hygienic—was one in which Wilde was particularly interested.)

II, 403–6   *I think . . . she is* In HTC this speech is much shorter:

I'm in love with Cecily. (*Enter* CECILY, *L. She picks up can and begins to water flowers, L.*) I must see Cecily before I go. Ah, there she is.   *Goes up & L.*

Then Alexander has stage-business with a watering-can throughout the sequence following. As Algernon approaches (l. 407), Cecily '*starts, turns round with can in her hands, sprinkles* ALGERNON *who rubs his clothes down with his handkerchief*'. At l. 409 he '*Takes hold of her hand which holds can*' and at l. 412 '*As* CECILY *moves down L. she leaves can in* ALGIE's *R. hand. He puts it behind tree*'. This develops business barely indicated in the HTC1 typescript: it is absent from French's edition (?1903) but the British Theatre Museum prompt-book, which is based on this French's edition and dates from the 1900s, restores it. LC omits ll. 394–413 ('Well, at any rate . . . afraid so').

II, 407   At this point the 3-act versions move to material originally placed near the beginning of Act III. In the MS draft Wilde had not decided how to get Jack off the stage and Cecily back on: the argument between Jack and Algernon is followed directly by a conversation in which Algernon proposes going to join the others at lunch and Cecily reproaches him with having tried to make Jack pay his debt to the Savoy. Algernon claims that the meals at the Savoy were for Bunbury, whose doctors will not allow him to eat anything but late suppers. (Cecily remarks, 'I don't wonder then that Mr. Bunbury is always so ill, if he

eats supper for six people every night of the week'.)
She has provided lunch for Algernon:

> . . . As you said you thought roast mutton too rich for you
> I told the butler to bring you lobsters.

ALGERNON

> Lobsters!

CECILY

> Yes, six lobsters. Those are all the lobsters we seem to
> have in the house, I am sorry to say. Of course if we had
> known you were coming we would have asked the house-
> keeper to order twelve.

ALGERNON

> I assure you six is quite enough. I never eat more than six
> lobsters for lunch.

CECILY

> I am glad to hear you are not so greedy as Miss Prism and
> dear Doctor Chasuble seem to think you.

Cecily hints to Jack that a ruse to get rid of Miss
Prism might be appropriate, and he decides to adopt
her plan and tell the governess that Dr Chasuble is
waiting for her somewhere. Jack returns, to tell
Algernon he must go, and Cecily stands in front of
the lobsters:

JACK

> What is behind you, Cecily? What are you trying to
> conceal?

CECILY

> Nothing, Uncle Jack. I have no past of any kind. That is
> the great drawback of living in the country. It puts one at
> such a disadvantage with other girls.

At the beginning of Act III Miss Prism and Cecily are
at work in the sitting-room. Algernon arrives and
tells her his white lie: Dr Chasuble is waiting for her
in the vestry. Cecily points out that the vestry is
excessively damp.

MISS PRISM

> True! I had not thought of that, and Dr Chasuble is sadly
> rheumatic. In spite of all that I can say he absolutely
> declines to wear flannels next the skin. I had better go at
> once. During my absence I trust you will proceed with
> your studies. The standard works on Political Economy
> are all here. If you wish for lighter reading you will find
> under my work-basket on that table a treatise on Physical
> Geography. It contains most interesting diagrams of the
> mountainous elevations of the world, drawn to scale and
> executed on copper plate.

After having her bonnet adjusted by Cecily, and reminding Algernon that as a man sows, so shall he reap, Miss Prism leaves, and the dialogue picks up with the equivalent of l. 413 in the present edition.

II, 708   *Hand that to Miss Fairfax* (om. HTC only) Alexander's s.d. for the tea-table sequence and his alterations to the HTC1 typescript show the evolution of the stage-business. In the typescript the women *'both put down their cups'* on the word 'cake' in l. 9 (the s.d. is not in LC). Alexander let this stand, but made it redundant by adding more elaborate business. When Merriman has left, Gwendolen comes over to the table and puts down her cup. Then she *'goes up to* CECILY *and holds out cake'* ('And though I asked most distinctly for bread and butter'). As she warns Cecily that she may go too far, she *'Bangs cake down on tray and goes R.*CECILY *comes down R.C.'* ('To save my poor, innocent trusting boy ...') and Gwendolen comes up to her to confront her ('From the moment I saw you ...'). In the British Theatre Museum prompt-book some of the s.d. in the French's text on which it is based have been revised to agree with HTC.

II, 891–2   *and there is still one muffin left* (om. HTC) Added to WD. The HTC1 typescript ends with s.d. 'JACK *groans and sinks onto settee'.* Like Wilde (in alterations to WD) Alexander alters the settee to a chair. In HTC business is added for a curtain-call: *'On second curtain,* JACK *takes tea-cakes;* ALGIE *takes it* [sic] *away, the same as he* [i.e. JACK] *starts to cut cake.* JACK *rises, comes over to garden seat to filch them'.* French's 1903 edition contains additional lines, which also appear in a typescript made for Frohman (possibly some time after the 1895 New York production) and now in New York Public Library at the Lincoln Center (+NCOF 1895):

ALGY *(sits R.C.)*
   I haven't quite finished my tea yet.
   Ring curtain down. ALGY *sits back of table and takes* JACK*'s cup of tea and begins to drink it*
JACK
   You are drinking my tea.
ALGY
   It's not your tea—you are eating my muffins—

JACK
They are not your muffins—
Curtain down by this. JACK *groans and sinks onto settee*

III, 76–82   *Her unhappy father ... But of course* (om. HTC)
HTC1 and earlier texts omit 'on the Influence of a
permanent income on Thought' and 'Indeed I have
never undeceived him on any question. I would consider it wrong'. The insertion of the lecture-title
compensates for the loss of a passage drafted for Act
I, referring to Gwendolen's attendance at University
Extension Scheme lectures ('I never return from one
... without having been excessively admired') and
Algernon's assertion (four speeches later in the same
passage) that she and Jack share an interest in such
questions as 'Better housing of the upper classes' and
'The bringing of Culture within the easy reach of the
rich'. The University of London's Extension Scheme
was a pioneer among extramural departments.

III, 97–106   *Oh! I killed ... so Bunbury died* HTC1 and LC cut
ll. 101–3 and the first phrase of l. 104 ('My dear Aunt
Augusta'). Alexander's version is even shorter, being
one speech for Algernon:

> Oh! Bunbury, he has quite exploded. I mean I killed
> Bunbury this afternoon. I mean poor Bunbury died this
> afternoon. I should say, the doctors found out that
> Bunbury could not live, so poor Bunbury died.

In the longer version of the passage found in the MS
draft and Arents IV, Lady Brancaster expresses surprise that Bunbury was 'a sufficiently eminent politi-
cian to be entitled to be in any way the object of
revolutionary outrages'. Algernon explains that
Bunbury was very useful in his way, but 'is not
necessary any more':

> Well, you bear his loss with wonderful equanimity, con-
> sidering the devotion you displayed to him during his
> lifetime. I am glad to have the opportunity of noting that
> in that respect you take after my side of the family. I
> never indulge in useless regrets of any kind. They seem to
> me morbid ...

The trial of the Walsall anarchists in 1892 and a series
of incidents involving explosives on the Continent

and (in 1894) in London had established political assassination in the public consciousness.

III, 175–80   *No, the side view ... just at present* 1899, HTC1, etc. (om. HTC only) In LC and earlier texts the passage is slightly different:

> ... There are *distinct* social possibilities in your profile.
> CECILY
> Really, Lady Brancaster? How very gratifying!
> LADY BRANCASTER
> Child! Never fall into the habit, so unfortunately common nowadays, of talking trivially about serious things. The two weak points ...

Wilde seems to have thought that this idea had been well enough established elsewhere. For *profile* (pronounced *pro-feel*, with the second syllable stressed) cf. 'Phrases and Philosophies for the Use of the Young' (*Chameleon*, December 1894):

> If the poor only had profiles there would be no difficulty in solving the problem of poverty ... There is something tragic about the enormous number of young men there are in England at the present moment who start life with perfect profiles, and end by adopting some useful profession.

> (*CW*, pp. 1205–6)

III, 238   The MS draft and Arents IV Cecily protests that Jack claimed untruthfully to have a brother. He insists that he has only been *inventing*:

> To invent anything at all is an act of sheer genius, and, in a commercial age like ours, shows considerable physical courage—Few of our modern novelists ever dare to invent a single thing. It is an open secret that they don't ·know how to do it.

Algernon, on the other hand, has *corroborated* an untruth, which is 'not the act of a gentleman'. Jack tells of the debt he has paid for Algernon, then, changing his tack, protests indignantly that Algernon has obliged him to pay his own bills:

> More young men are ruined nowadays by paying their bills than by anything else. I know many fashionable young men in London, young men of rank and position, whose rooms are absolutely littered with receipts, and who, with a callousness that seems to me absolutely

cynical, have no hesitation in paying ready money for the mere luxuries of life. Such conduct seems to me to strike at the very foundation of things. The only basis for good Society is unlimited credit. Without that, Society, as we know it, crumbles. Why is it that we all despise the middle classes? Simply because they invariably pay what they owe . . .

Lady Brancaster insists that she will overlook her nephew's conduct. Cecily argues with Jack, but he will not respond ('Guardians, like judges, curates, and people in high authority never argue. It is safer, and more impressive'). Only the first three speeches of this sequence (on lying and corroborating) appear in LC. By WD the whole passage has been discarded.

III, 429–30 *Well . . . practice* 1899 (om. HTC only; HTC1, etc. om. second sentence) In LC and earlier texts this is followed by a passage in which Miss Prism tenders her resignation, apologizing to Jack for her negligent treatment of him. She has nothing more to teach Cecily: 'In the very difficult accomplishment of getting married I fear my sweet and clever pupil has far outstripped her teacher'. Dr Chasuble takes the hint and intervenes—he has 'come to the conclusion that the Primitive Church was in error on certain points. Corrupt readings seem to have crept into the text'. He offers her his hand in marriage. Laetitia tells Frederick (they are on first-name terms now) that she is unable to express her feelings, but will send him the three volumes of her diary so that he will be able to peruse a full account of her feelings towards him for the past eight months. Merriman announces that Lady Brancaster's flyman cannot wait any longer: she and Gwendolen have missed nine trains and there is only one more. She leaves the company with good wishes and advice—Miss Prism, she hopes, will be more careful of her husband than she had been of Jack,

. . . and not leave poor Dr Chasuble lying about at railway stations in hand-bags or receptacles of any kind. Cloakrooms are notoriously draughty places.

Dr Chasuble would do well to have Miss Prism christened without delay. (In the MS version of Miss Prism's contrite apologies she admits 'It had never occurred to me before that as a woman sows, so shall she reap. I had thought that aphorism only applied to the male sex'.)

III, 458–72 *His name ... I mean it naturally is Ernest* 1899, HTC1 (om. HTC only) In HTC1 Maxbohm (a reference to Max Beerbohm) and Magley are not included in the list of Generals and 1860 (as in earlier texts) is the year of Moncrieff's promotion. The changes were made in revisions to WD. In the MS draft and Arents IV Jack distributes volumes among the others, but Dr Chasuble has been given the 1869 edition of Bradshaw's Railway Guide, Cecily a copy of Justin McCarthy's popular *History of Our Own Times*, and Miss Prism two copies of the price list of the Civil Service Stores (a department store for members of that body)—Generals are nowhere listed and appear to be either in little demand or poor supply. To Arents IV Wilde adds a speech for Lady Bracknell, who has been given a copy of Hichens's satire *The Green Carnation* (in which Wilde and Douglas had been lampooned): it 'seems to be a book about the culture of exotics. It contains no reference to Generals in it [*sic*]. It seems to be a morbid and middle class affair'. The distribution, but not the reactions to the books, was preserved in LC and then abandoned.